Living Catholic Faith in a Contentious Age

LIVING CATHOLIC FAITH IN A CONTENTIOUS AGE

Raymond G. Helmick, S.J.

continuum

Continuum International Publishing Group
The Tower Building, 11 York Road, London, SE1 7NX
80 Maiden Lane, Suite 704, New York, NY 10038

www.continuumbooks.com

British Library Cataloguing-in-Publication Data
A catalogue record for this book is available from the British Library

Typeset by Pindar NZ, Auckland, New Zealand
Printed and bound in Great Britain by the MPG Books Group

ISBN: 978-1-4411-5219-0 (Paperback)

Contents

Foreword

In his wonderful work *The Rise of Christianity*, Rodney Stark argues that contrary to romanticized notions about the early flourishing of Christianity, the new religion was an urban movement. Christianity rose because urban areas were dreadful. Stark describes their conditions as "social chaos and chronic urban misery." Sheer population density exacerbated the situation. At the end of the first century, Antioch's population was 150,000 within the city walls—117 persons per acre. New York City today has a density of 37 persons per acre overall; Manhattan, with its high-rise apartments, registers 100 persons per acre.

Contrary to early assumptions, Greco-Roman cities were not settled places, made up of inhabitants descending from previous generations. Given high infant mortality and short life expectancy, these cities required a constant, substantial stream of newcomers simply to maintain population levels. As a result, the cities were comprised of strangers. These strangers were well treated by Christians who, again contrary to assumptions, were certainly not universally poor. Through a variety of ways, financially secure Christians mercifully welcomed the newly arrived immigrants. Indeed, if mercy is, as I argue, the willingness to enter into the chaos of another, the church was merciful from its inception.

Moreover, Christianity was new. While ethical demands were imposed by the gods of the pagan religions, these demands were substantively ritualistic, not neighbor directed. And, while pagan Romans knew generosity, it did not stem from any divine command. Thus a nurse who cared for a victim of an epidemic knew that her life might be lost. If she were a pagan, there was no expectation of divine reward for her generosity; if she were a Christian, this life was but a prelude to the next, where the generous were united with God.

Although Romans practiced generosity, they did not promote mercy or pity. Since mercy implied "unearned help or relief," it was considered contradictory to justice. Roman philosophers opposed mercy. Pity was a defect of character, belonging to the uneducated and the naïve. Stark concludes:

> This was the moral climate in which Christianity taught that mercy is one of the primary virtues—that a merciful God requires humans to be merciful. Moreover, the corollary that because God loves humanity, Christians may not please God unless they love one another was entirely new. Perhaps even more revolutionary was the principle that Christian love and charity must extend beyond the boundaries of family and tribe, that it must extend to "all those who in every place call on the name of our Lord Jesus Christ" (1 Corinthians 1.2).

This was revolutionary stuff. Indeed, it was the cultural basis for the revitalization of a Roman world groaning under a host of miseries. (212)

Christianity has often been known for its merciful generosity. The entire health care system in the west was developed from the hospitable communities of faith. Similarly, education and social services finds their roots in early Christian initiatives. The care for the prisoner, the homeless, and the hungry as well as for the widow and the orphan was always a trait of Christianity. Today, Catholic health care, social services, and educational institutions thrive in their service and mission as they have for centuries.

As outgoing and caring as Christians are, they can also be contentious. Think for a moment about the early, first century church at the Council of Jerusalem (*Acts 15*) where the leaders debated the question of circumcision and other Jewish purity rituals. This was not a simple amicable gathering. The debates preceding the council about baptizing Gentiles had to have sown seeds of contention, which inevitably were outsourced by differing forms of authority. Not surprisingly, early communities were in themselves contentious; we can think here of Paul addressing the Corinthians about their scandalous fractions that pervaded that local church. Or, think of what early Christian meals must have been like that they required the creation of the office of deacon to serve the neglected widows.

The call to be merciful was often well answered by the

church and its members; the summons to avoid contention was, well, less heard. In some instances, the deafness to the summons is rather startling. Consider the case of Cardinal Bartolome Carranza (1503–1576). Carranza entered the Dominicans at seventeen and by the age of twenty-four was a leading theologian.

Charles V sent him to the Council of Trent. In 1558 Charles' son Philip appointed him archbishop of Toledo and primate of all Spain. In the same year, he was denounced to the Inquisition for his commentary on the Catechism even though five years later in 1563 it was approved by a commission from the Council of Trent. Still, in 1559 Philip had Carranza arrested. Carranza remained in prison without a trial for eight years. Carranza appealed to Rome, which granted his hearing, but first incarcerated him in the Castel St. Angelo for ten years. Though he was acquitted of heresy, he died six days after his release.

Carranza was denounced by the other major Spanish Dominican theologian of his time, Melchior Cano. On the other hand another Dominican Luis de Granada and the first Jesuit cardinal, Francesco de Toledo were his defenders. But the Carranza case was a contentious one, where some feared another's contribution as suspect and others believed that his accusers were abusing the tradition.

The case of Carranza belongs to a litany of contentious cases in the church because such contention occurs when measured attempts at innovation are met with intolerance. This is not to suggest that intolerance arises from a simple dispositional intransigence; rather it arises because sometimes, rightfully or not, we find another's contribution a threat to our own understanding of how the tradition ought to be expressed. And these threats are from both sides of the aisle.

This is a perennial affair, all too familiar, and one not at all limited to Catholics. In a striking essay the Orthodox theologian Vigen Guroian discussed a fairly acrimonious debate about Christology within the Armenia church in which, as Guroian notes, civility failed ("Doctrine and Ecclesial Authority: A Contemporary Controversy in the Armenian Church," James F. Keenan and Joseph Kotva, eds. *Practice What You Preach*, Franklin, WI: Sheed and Ward, 1999, 252-67).

Of course all such contentious moments are clear evidence of the failure of the church to be what it is called to be. In our own day, contention is as much as a scandal as it has always been. And it arises every time we fail to see the necessary connection between a living, yet long-standing tradition and the actual diverse expectations of the community of faith.

There are a variety of approaches to address this contentiousness. Those in authoritative office might try to engender greater unity and understanding precisely in the midst of evident tensions. Canon lawyers might offer ways to understand how the church's law procedurally addresses divisive issues in the church. Ethicists, as we did in the volume above, might turn to norms and virtues to suggest better ways for fostering personal and communal responsibility within the church. Theologians might reflect on the nature of the church and the sacrament of baptism as constitutive elements leading us to appreciation for the unity of the church.

In this work here, we have a completely new approach. Raymond G. Helmick, S.J., an internationally known and respected churchman, who has promoted throughout his entire life the practice of reconciliation, invites us into a meditation on the nature of Christian faith. He asks us to consider whether in *living that faith* we adequately appreciate that faith saves not only us, but others. We are invited to believe not only for our own salvation but so that the church may be a sacrament of faith, hope and charity for others. Do we compromise the faith of others as we fight with one another over our own?

Whether in Ulster, Kosovo, Beirut, or throughout the Mideast, Helmick has been an active witness to peace through reconciliation and forgiveness. All too aware of the limitations of our humanity, Helmick has a humble yet abiding hope in the possibility of humanity to understand the challenges of diverse traditions and to live respectfully with that diversity. A catalyst in so many negotiations for unity and peace, Helmick brings his own stance to reflect not on reconciliation or peace itself, but rather on faith. He is convinced that if we have true living faith in the true living God we can be a more united church and a witness to the love of God.

With a traditional assumption that faith must seek understanding, Helmick brings us into his meditation on how faith leads us to God through the church and her sacraments. This is not a theological treatise but rather a careful, thoughtful and concrete attempt to help us to see our faith today not as the source of conceptual and ideological division but rather as a gift that brings us to a humble understanding of ourselves and our church.

There is healing in these pages, precisely because a true living faith makes us merciful. For if mercy is the willingness to enter into the chaos of another, then mercy is the willingness to enter into the church as it is today. And living faith, as you will learn from Helmick, makes that mercy possible and sustainable.

James F. Keenan, S.J.
Founders Professor in Theology
Boston College
Christmas, 2009

Preface

The German philosopher, Friedrich Nietzsche, once declared as his own discovery the suggestion that all philosophy was thinly-disguised biography. And his own life and work were certainly no exceptions to this rule. I have long believed that something analogous might be said about theology. One need not go so far as the sweeping judgment offered by Nietzsche, but I think the biography, indeed the story and experiences as well as the context of theologians, are all vitally important in order to understand better the work of any particular theologian. And, of course, one cannot limit theology to the written and preached word alone for one of the great gifts of twentieth century theologising to history was the timely reminder that praxis is vitally important to all theology. Theologians were reminded of their responsibility to be 'doers of the word', and 'doing the truth' became as important a challenge as the more traditional ways of bearing witness to the faith. Orthopraxis returned to its rightful place alongside orthodoxy.

Now, of course, such a suggestion concerning the relationship between biography and theology is nothing new. We have four gospels which each reflect, in differing ways and from differing perspectives, upon the story of an extraordinary brief life in first century Palestine. The very notion of saints and their travails and triumphs alike bears testimony to the same hypothesis and, of course, who, when the name of Augustine of Hippo crops up, does not think instantly of his *Confessions*? Naturally others have reflected upon such a connection between theology and biography, between the lives of the people who speak, write and act in theological ways, in more recent years. To take but one example, in 2005, it was delightful to see a wonderful collection published which appeared to confirm this hunch further and brought together theologians from very different backgrounds and asked them to reflect upon their own story and how this had impacted upon their own work.[1]

None of this may be particularly surprising to a Jesuit, of course, for the Society of Jesus has always laid great emphasis upon action – putting faith into practice. One of the most wonderful anthologies of the numerous works by the great German Jesuit, Karl Rahner, is called *The Practice of Faith* and each century - especially the last century - offers rich examples of Jesuits who have lived out their vows and commitment to the faith, not least of all Saint Ignatius, himself and his own biography has proved especially inspiring. The imperatival importance of doing theology, of living the faith is something which so many Jesuits throughout history appear to take as a non-negotiable given.

---

1   Gesa E. Thiessen and Declan Marmion, *Theology in the Making*, Dublin, Veritas, 2005.

This all might serve as an all too brief prologue to discerning the immense value and importance of this present volume, for the book which you hold in your hands is a true gem which I promise will leave you inspired to action and will provoke your thoughts for a very long time after you turn the final page. And this is true not least of all because Ray Helmick's *Living Catholic Faith in a Contentious Age* is an extraordinary work which helps demonstrate how personal story, how a lifetime's work and experiences of a theologian and servant of the church can help offer so many valuable insights and lessons to a church which is going through troubled times, mirroring the wider world which is always fully present in the church as much as the church is always fully present in and part of the world that is God's own creation.

So much of Ray Helmick's life has been spent working in the midst of some of the most dreadful conflicts that history will recall. What he does in this book is bring all the experiences and wisdom gained through living so much of his life as a peacemaker in the eye of the storm home to his own church, currently so much in need of reconciliation itself. His book, then, draws upon his immense experience in working with wounded communities in order to try and offer guidance to what is patently a 'wounded church', as chapter one describes.

Ray Helmick has crafted for us a systematic study that progresses towards addressing the heart of the issues that each chapter is concerned with, and in a practical way. This is a volume which addresses questions of global importance within and without the Christian church. The most pressing questions and divisions concerning inter-faith and inter-church relations, the essential elements of the faith, the nature and responsibilities of theology itself, the meanings of 'orthodoxy', the complexities of human sexuality, power, authority and governance are all addressed throughout its pages. Even the more obviously theological chapters pave the way for an unleashing of the theological vision behind them in terms of the 'real world'. As a true Jesuit, Helmick begins with some serious and stimulating reflections upon the dynamics of the relationship between the individual Christian, God and the church (in that order). The final chapter – fitting in the extreme given the focus of the foregoing chapters – is a fascinating account of the particular context of so much of Helmick's own work working for the overcoming of conflict and reconciliation of deeply divided communities in places such as the Middle East and Northern Ireland. But it offers lessons of much wider relevance for the wounded church and our wider societies alike.

Few would try to suggest that there have been deep divisions and serious errors, as well as wrongdoings within the church in recent decades and within our wider societies alike. Drawing upon his experiences in societies ravaged by conflict, Ray Helmick does not pull any punches in pointing out where such things have taken place, nor in suggesting the organizational fault lines within the church and beyond which have led to and then further compounded the same. But, in each case, Helmick wishes to work towards a distinctly positive conclusion.

There are so many different ways in which the chapters here will touch different people. In one sense, the biographical elements alone would make this the most enthralling read. But the long years of dedicated service to the church and the wider communities and societies in which the church is called to live out its existence that Ray Helmick has given have not only borne rich fruit in each of the many places and challenging situations in which he has found himself working. Those years of selfless commitment have offered and will continue to offer invaluable lessons for all people of good will who come into contact with this story, these insights and, of course, with their author.

But I do not wish to give the impression that this is a work of biographical reflection – far from it. Rather I wish to underline just how much richer the theological, ethical, ecclesiological, inter-faith and ecumenical reflections you have before you actually are because of the story behind the author who offers them.

This is an incredibly brave book. It takes courage to offer theological and moral reflections upon some of the greatest challenges that have faced the churches in recent decades and some of the most pressing and divisive situations that have enveloped much wider communities, still.

Ray Helmick does not fear to criticize any party, faction, viewpoint or practice within that church that does not build up the whole, regardless of office or power. Such a stance, drawn from those decades of experience in situations of conflict and strife, is important. Speaking to intra-Catholic implications, I believe it would take an especially misguided ecclesial perception, lacking all sense of irony to raise objections to such a book which cuts to the heart of the malaises concerning power, authority and accountability within the current church. Instead, this volume should be required reading for priests, religious, prelates, curial and diocesan officials alike, as well as, of course, theologians and pastoral workers, in order that they might humbly learn how problems within the church have come about, their complicity within such and how to ensure, through a process of penance, humility and reconciliation, that lessons are learned honestly and openly and that the future may be more brighter than recent times.

Such are my own views, of course, but the joy of this work is that Ray Helmick does not seek to browbeat and to criticize for the sake of comment – to do so would be all too easy. Instead, he seeks to be constructive, inspiring, to offer ways forward for a church and societies ravaged by division, by hurt, by controversy, by sinful silence and omissions. Above all else, this is a book which bears testimony to the power of hope.

Not only does this volume offer an engagement with the most important challenges facing the Catholic church in recent times. This book will also appeal to those working in and with the church, to academic scholars, students and ministerial candidates alike. So, too, will those working in ecumenical organisations and campaigns and in the areas of inter-religious and inter-cultural dialogue, as well as in conflict resolution and reconciliation. Because it spans the broad fields of ecclesiology, moral, political and public theology alike, it should generate significant conversation and debate.

There are numerous popular volumes addressing the contemporary challenges for the church today, but this text is something very different in the unswerving commitment to applying the experiences and practices and methods pertaining to conflict resolution and community building to the contemporary church and ecclesiological context.

Overall, it is an accessible, reflective and moving text that captures the imagination and attempts to transcend the polemic that has plagued the church in recent decades in a most constructive fashion.

Within these pages you will find truly prophetic words – in every sense of the meaning of that word. This book is the voice of a member of the Society of Jesus, a priest, following his calling. It speaks uncomfortable truths to all of us – regardless of status, rank or power. And it reminds us that all division and conflict can be overcome if sincere and concerted efforts are offered by those who can make a difference. Finally, it heralds the amazing transformative power of faith, hope and love – that the truth can overcome the darkness of the darkest situations. In the call for a new and more inclusive church council, a genuinely ecumenical council, the prophetic nature of these pages might find their lasting legacy. Forgiveness and reconciliation run throughout its pages as abiding imperatives for us all. A biographical hermeneutic, then, is the key to this rich and highly commendable contribution to discerning a better way for the church of tomorrow.

Gerard Mannion
House Sylvius, Jezuïetenhof, Wijgmaal, nr Leuven
Feast of St Francis Xavier, 2009

Introduction

We Catholics in the United States have fallen out of sorts with one another in recent years. This may appear to be largely a matter of civility, of which we see rather little in our conduct toward one another, but at a deeper level it reflects deep differences of outlook that have a profoundly theological dimension. Is our faith truly placed in God, who has revealed himself? And is our conduct toward one another genuinely Christian?

The annual Summer Institute for Priests held by the International Institute for Clergy Formation at Seton Hall University gave me the opportunity, a few years ago, to ask these questions and to put them into the context of faith: Christian and Catholic faith. My title speaks of living that Catholic faith, and this is not merely a matter of beliefs, of which doctrinal propositions we affirm, but, much more importantly, how we conduct our lives.

We have our calling as Church, as the community of faith, not merely for our own salvation, but in order that we may be the face of Christ in the world; the evidence, by reason of the way we live, to all those who are not of our community that the Lord is present and active in our world and theirs. Our task as

1

a communion, the Communion of Saints, is to witness to that presence. Christ himself, coming among us as one of ourselves, was in his person the manifestation of that presence of God among us that God had always promised. For us, the Church, as Body of Christ, it is our manner of living that counts, more than anything else we may say or do.

Beset with our culture wars, we have made ourselves very vulnerable to false objects of faith. Holding fast to our doctrinal positions, liberal or conservative, supplies us with our sense of identity and loyalty to our faction in Catholicism; or even, if we rise above this factionalism, to the Church as such, representing our belonging to the long tradition of Christian faith. This gives us a niche, a sense of security, and our faithfulness to a set of creedal positions can itself become the object of our faith. But it can offer no genuine substitute for the true object of faith, God himself, in whom we can put our full trust, orienting our lives confidently to the promises he has made to us.

I begin this study, therefore, by identifying God as the object of faith proclaimed throughout the scriptural record of his self-revelation. The good news which God tells us is that we can put our faith in him, that we can live without fear and with courage because he is with us. Here is the living centre of his revelation of himself to his chosen Jewish people, and in this we find the very substance of our life as disciples of Christ, who, by coming among us, has shown us the Father and his love for us. I hope this may help to ground our understanding of the living process of faith and cast some critical light on the way we have been treating one another within the Catholic faith community in recent years.

Theology itself has been at the heart of our discontents with one another. Many of our Catholics, including many of our bishops, have had a fear of theology as a discipline that can interfere with their certitudes and complicate their lives of faith. A second chapter consequently asks about the theologian's task, and seeks the answer in the traditional definition of theology given by St Augustine, and echoed centuries later by St Anselm — that it is faith in search of understanding. Our statements of belief, always inadequate efforts to formulate the content of our faith in ways that can express faithfully our understanding of it, have constant need of fresh interpretation.

As we have struggled among ourselves as Catholics in these years, particular emphasis has been given to the orthodoxy of teaching, especially that of theologians. Chapter 3 turns to the nature of orthodoxy, which cannot be a matter simply of always having the right answers. None of us has those, none of us is always right, but we have, as part of our revelation, the promise that the Holy Spirit will lead us into all truth. Where and how are we to find this Spirit and follow his leading?

With Chapter 4 we look at the degree of polarization in our Church — an angry Right that is always looking for loyalty tests on wedge issues and an equally angry Left that is disillusioned with Church leadership and defiant — and ask how we are to overcome it. So much of the strident partisan rivalry within our Church represents the quest for power over others, whether coming from the Right or from the Left. Once our striving is basically to exert control over others, it may be posed in terms of doctrinal positions, for some of absolutism, for others of freedom, but in fact it has little if anything to do with faith. Certainly such an atmosphere of strife and rejection does not witness to faith as a way of living in imitation of Christ, the merciful and forgiving, whose first concern is for the sheep that is lost.

These contests were at full throttle even before the Catholic Church was rocked by the sexual abuse scandals that came to light early in 2002. But in the atmosphere of disgust and suspicion that those sorry disclosures generated, the breakdown of civility has reached the proportions of guerrilla warfare, either side anxious to discredit the other, to break down the other's institutional structures. The already existing crisis of institutional trust within the Church reached, at this point, Reformation proportions. Many of our hierarchy are anxious to 'put this behind them', and try to assure themselves that the worst is now past. It has been my own contention that the shock to the Church is still with us and, if not addressed directly, has the potential to be as lastingly divisive of our unity as Church as was the sixteenth century crisis. The Church then responded, for the most part, defensively.

In Chapter 5, therefore, I argue that we cannot afford to do that again and that we can best address the central problems this crisis has revealed at the level of a new Council of the Church. I see those central problems as, first, a crudely inadequate view of human sexuality, one with no Christian credentials yet which has wide prevalence among both Protestant and Catholic Christians and, second, the vexed question of accountability within the Church. Neither of those has ever been addressed directly at the level of a Council, and they both now hang menacingly over our Church.

So much of our belligerency goes back to our contentious history as a Church that has divided repeatedly, solving our quarrels by rejection and dismissal of other Christians, to the disruption of the unity for which Christ prayed. Chapter 6 addresses this ecumenical question at the level of sacramental disunity, our inability to share our sacramental life.

As conclusion, Chapter 7 takes up the work of forgiveness and reconciliation as a fundamental dimension of the mission of the Church.

CHAPTER 1

Catholic Faith: How We Relate to God and Church

'Lord, may this Eucharist accomplish in your Church the unity and peace it signifies. Grant this through Christ our Lord. Amen.' We say this simple prayer after communion in the Masses of the 11th Week in Ordinary Time, the week in which I write these opening thoughts on Catholic faith. And it is in the sharing of the Eucharist that we most consciously symbolize and live our Catholic commitment.

We have made a terrible job of unity throughout the history of the Church. We pray a lot now for Christian unity, with so much left to repair after all the centuries in which we gave it little care. But peace, too, has become remote from us as we have conducted what seems much like civil war in our churches. Nearly all the Reformation churches find themselves entangled these days in fierce internal battles over matters of human sexuality. We have those battles ourselves, as Catholics, but the

7

main field of our contention seems much deeper, about faith itself. Catholics fully committed to a life of faith look upon one another with real hostility, regarding each other's faith as suspect. The cutting edge of this is fidelity to the Church, and it is here that we have doubts about one another, setting loyalty tests.

SOURCES OF CONFLICT

Christians of every sort regard the Church as vital to their practice of faith. Reducing faith to a privatized God-and-me relation always seems a poor substitute for a life in communion of faith with others. We live in constant conversation and exchange with one another, sharing much in our lives. It is a lonely life to be without this, and to be unable to communicate with others about something so important to our lives as faith – if we happen to have it – means painful deprivation.

For Catholics, the sense of Church as authority tends to overshadow this wider concept of Church as fellowship or communion in faith. For the Catholic it has great importance to be at one with a central teaching authority in the Church. Much has happened in recent times to shake the confidence of many Catholics in that authoritative centre, but for others any questioning of that centre equates with disloyalty to the faith. And that is our civil war.

In part this is very recent. We are a wounded Church these

days. A process of secularization had already proceeded far in our American society, removing many of the external societal props that made it a matter of course for Catholics, or any other Christians, to be regular churchgoers, before the scandals of the new millennium hit us. The disillusionment that sprang from the spectacle of priests sexually abusing altar boys and other young people, and their bishops appearing more concerned to look innocent than to address the subject, has left a great many of our Catholic people adrift, reckoning the Church irrelevant even to the best, most generous concerns of their lives. In the face of troubles, they then wonder what they can really rely on. That is a faith question. We may, even if we are regular churchgoers, be looking for alternative objects of faith that we can rely on: governments, 'forces of order', friends in high places, whatever would make us safe, or safer than we would be without them.

We see opinion polls listing the degree of trust the public invests in various institutions – government, the President, Congress, political parties, the press, schools, churches, etc. Churches, bishops, and clergy now rank pretty low. Sunday attendance falls, and its importance, in the minds of increasing numbers of our people, shrinks. The question that the press used to ask regularly – what has the Church to say on any given subject, even if it is on one of the grand moral topics – evokes little interest. People have come to expect that the Church, when asked such questions, will answer only in a way that supports its institutional interests, and even with the best of good will that does not impress us as very important.

This, of course, reflects an understanding of Church which identifies it essentially as its teaching core, not the broader definition of Church as the people of God which was emphasized by the Second Vatican Council. But the continued existence of so radical a difference in the understanding of Church points, to an underlying distrust, on the part of those whose concepts of the Church and of Catholic faith predate that Council, of the Council itself and the directions in which it has led the Church. Catholics such as these, fearful of what they see as a Protestantizing of the Church and more anxious to stress Catholic difference than to recognize community of faith with other Christians, have been comforted by the signs of restorationism in the years since the Council; the tendency to pull the Church back toward its former state. But now they, too, are heartsick at the revelations of abuse that they have heard in recent years, and wondering who is to be blamed. It is a great time for scapegoating.

IN WHAT DO WE PLACE OUR FAITH?

All of that is more a sociological look at the Church than an examination of its faith. But faith, if we have it, affects us at a far deeper level.

That 'if we have it' proviso is essential to the question, as the person of faith is at home in the world, confident in the meaning of life, able to live and act with assurance in the face of the perils that are all about us. Many of us have great difficulty in doing that. We may be striving for faith, in the honest situation of the man who tells Jesus: 'Lord, I believe, help my unbelief' (Mark 9.24). Faith, though not a terribly complicated thing, can be difficult for any of us in our alarming world.

Assent to a text is not the issue here, but rather a commitment to that in which we place our faith, a commitment which will be manifested in action rather than simply in a profession. Jesus, in the Gospels, recognizes the faith of many persons: the Centurion who pleads for his servant (Matthew 8.10, Luke 7.9), the friends who bring a paralytic to him to be healed (Matthew 9.2, Mark 2.5, Luke 5.20), the woman with haemorrhage who touches his garment (Matthew 9.22, Mark 5.34, Luke 8.48), the two blind men who follow him asking for their sight (Matthew 9.29), blind Bartimaeus (Mark 10.52, Luke 18.42), the Canaanite woman who seeks healing for her daughter (Matthew 15.28), the sinful woman who washes his feet (Luke 7.50), the one leper among ten who returns to give thanks for his cure (Luke 17.19). Some of these are not of the Jewish community of faith, but all come to him in confidence that he will heal them. Of the Centurion he says: 'Such faith I have not found in Israel'. So he is not looking strictly at adherence to a creed.

I do this with Scripture references, but it is our own basic experience that we can recognize here. Abraham believed God and it was reckoned to him as righteousness (Roman 4.3,

Galatians 3.6). His belief was in God's promise. And we 'in Jesus Christ [are] sons (and daughters) of God through faith' (Galatians 3.26). Our faith is in God and in Christ.

And then there is the Church. Our Creed, whether we use the Nicaean or the Apostles' Creed, states it plainly: we believe — we place our faith — in God, in one God. It elaborates on what we know of God — Father, Son, Holy Spirit, their relations and their actions toward us. And then it says, 'We believe in one holy, catholic and apostolic church'. Object of faith. But how?

This brings us right back to the different concepts of Church. When the Creed speaks of Church, it does so in the context of the teaching on the Holy Spirit. In some of the earliest creedal formulas the phrasing is even that 'we believe in the Holy Spirit in the Holy Church'. It is in the Church that we encounter the Spirit. Is it that we encounter the Spirit in the authoritative teaching of the Church? Surely this is an aspect of our Catholic conviction, and the one that is so much under challenge now in our crisis of confidence. But is it not primarily that we encounter the Spirit present among us in the communion of faith? Here is the promise, that Christ will not leave us orphans (John 14.18), but that the Spirit whom he sends will live among us, teaching us (John 14.26), guiding us into all truth (John 16.13). The Lord is with us: in the communion of faith.

The creed has nothing to say about the Eucharist, which has shown itself so much the focus of our faith, doubtless because this was uncontested at the time the creed was formulated. But surely it is here, joined together in the Eucharist as Body of Christ, that we have experience of the Church faith community, as object of faith. Objects of faith must in some way partake of God, as does everything in the creed without exception. The many articles of the creed unpack our understanding of what it means that we believe in God. Otherwise they would constitute alternatives to him as objects of faith.

God's actual dealing with us is in community, his teaching about our relationships to him and to one another. We are conscious always of our needs. The Psalms, which connect us with the life of prayer of the Jewish faith community and which were the prayers of Jesus, are always full of our needs. We turn to God with them, and we help one another to deal with them. The needs are profound, and we may express them differently. The Eastern Church traditionally fixes its attention on our needs in the face of death. God responds to this, bringing us life, and we see prominent in every Orthodox church the symbol of this promise, the figure of Christ, ruler of all things, the Pantocrator. The Western Church looks first to the dilemma of our sinfulness, the ruin we so regularly bring upon ourselves, and we know that God's response to it is forgiveness. The cross is its symbol, and is visible in every church.

SCRIPTURAL PRESENTATION OF FAITH

The scriptural witness testifies always to God as object of our faith. It shows us always God revealing himself, not as the distant abstraction of the philosophers but as acting in deed and word on our behalf. Running as a thread throughout the Hebrew Bible is a sequence of expressions that urge us to faith in God in terms of vast assurance:

> The Lord speaks:
> Do not fear. Do not be alarmed.
> Take courage. Take heart.
> Because I am with you.

This is the very stuff that faith is made of, and it occurs so constantly in the Scripture as to be much more than just a refrain. Wherever we find this sequence it is the Lord who speaks. It amounts practically to a signature, and becomes as well a principal element in the content of what the Lord says to us. We can rely on him. We can face life and all its vicissitudes with courage and without fear, because he is with us.

Hebrew language characteristically often doubles its expressions: 'Do not fear, do not be alarmed'. 'Take courage, take heart'. When we find this formula, it includes sometimes all these terms, sometimes more or less of them, but it remains recognizable in its many forms.

The assurance of the Lord's presence may be in an event that shows him. The formula occurs often in the context, always a problematic one for us, of Holy War, as in the books of Deuteronomy (e.g., ch. 20, the most basic passage, laying down the rules for Holy War, or ch. 7, 16–21), Numbers (ch. 21, where Moses does battle with Og, King of Bashan, or ch. 14, dealing with the people's rebellion in the desert) and Joshua (ch. 8, as Joshua confronts the king of Ai; ch. 10, before and after the battle with the five Amorite kings at Gibeon, vv. 8 and 25; ch. 11, 6–8, before his battle with the kings confederated under Jabin), echoed further in Judges (the Gideon story, ch. 7, where the Lord insists that Gideon reduce his forces to just a few against the massed troops of the Midianites, showing that it is he himself who defeats them) and even in the later historical books. In these instances, the final assurance often takes the form: 'I will deliver your enemy into your hands'.

We have in our time a well-founded allergy to the very concept of Holy War, and this frequent usage often seems a direct contradiction to the Scripture's message of peace. It causes serious distress when we find that the most belligerent of Israeli settlers invoke it to justify violent incursions against their Palestinian neighbours, so much so that Israeli peace activists shrink from the use of these terms.

But this is far from the principal context of these words of promise and assurance. We find them even more regularly in formulae of commission. They promise the Lord's presence and assistance when prophets (Gideon in Judges 6.11-24, Jeremiah 1.1-19, Ezekiel 2.1-3.12 and Daniel 10.1-11.1) or kings receive their calling, or when other persons are commissioned to perform great works, summoning them to reliance and trust. Such is the case with Joshua himself (Deuteronomy 31.7-8, as Moses addresses him, and again Deuteronomy 31.23 and

Joshua 1.6-9, as God himself speaks). David (1 Chronicles 22) receives his commission to gather the materials for the temple in these terms, as does Solomon (1 Chronicles 28) for the actual building of the temple. And when the people return from the exile, the Lord summons them to rebuild the temple in the same language (Haggai 2.1-9).

But the most telling appeals to faith in these terms occur in Isaiah, where these assurances, 'Have no fear, take courage, because I am with you', acquire the full character of prophecies of salvation. Isaiah 10.20-3, is the model for this, as the remnant of Israel is told that their redemption nears, that the Lord's wrath is turned away from them. On this basis, the Deutero-Isaiah builds the glowing messianic passages of chapters 35, 40, 41, 43, 44, 51 and 54 that are the staples of our Advent and Christmas liturgies and come back again in Lent and Easter. Jeremiah carries on this theme in his chapters 30 and 46, promising redemption from the exile. Joel (ch. 2, 18-27), Zephaniah (ch. 2) and Zechariah (ch. 8) follow in their steps, foretelling the Lord's coming in these same terms.

But the most important way in which this theme — have no fear, the Lord is with you — expresses the central faith meaning of the Hebrew Bible is in the Covenant texts of the book of Genesis. Each of the Patriarchs is addressed in these terms: Abraham (ch. 15, 1-6), Isaac (ch. 26, 24) and Jacob (ch. 46, 2-4). So also is Hagar, the mother of Ismael. Cast out from Abraham's house by the jealousy of Sarah, she despairs in the desert, believing that she and her son will perish, but the Lord speaks and gives her his assurance of her son's place in his plan (ch. 21, 17-18). In each case, the Covenant promises have already been made in other terms, but it appears to be a ritual necessity that they be repeated in the words of this formula, a kind of seal of God's faithfulness to them.

In Exodus 14, Moses addresses the people in these terms of reassurance when they fear the approaching Egyptians as they come to the Red Sea. He uses them again in chapter 20 as the people experience the fearful signs of God's presence at Mount Sinai. The Lord is not a reason to fear, but a reason to put away all fear.

These passages become a central expression of the appeal to put faith in God because of his actions toward his people. The strong and constant guarantee of his promises is surely funda-mental to the content of God's revelation. Their atmosphere shapes the whole context of the Psalms.

IN THE CHRISTIAN NEW TESTAMENT

The New Testament writers clearly recognize the centrality of these formulae. We find them especially throughout the Gospels. Both Matthew and Luke use them in the infancy nar-ratives to express the Lord's coming among us as man. Joseph hears these words in his dream (Matthew 1.18-23): 'Joseph, son of David, do not fear to take Mary as your wife, for that which is conceived in her is of the Holy Spirit'. Zachariah receives the promise of the birth of John the Baptist in this language (Luke 1.11-20) and the same terms, redolent of all those Hebrew Bible passages, return in the annunciation to Mary that she will bear the Child Jesus (Luke 1.26-38): 'The Lord is with you', she is told. The traditional form 'Take courage' is transformed into 'You shall have joy and gladness'. And because, like both Joseph and Zachariah, 'she was deeply troubled', the angel says to her, 'Do not fear, Mary'.

The promise of God's presence and assistance is then made very specific (v. 35): 'The Holy Spirit will come upon you, and the power of the Most High will overshadow you; for that reason the holy child to be born will be called Son of God'. And, as often happens in the Hebrew Bible, the promise of assistance is then buttressed by a miraculous sign: that Elizabeth, her cousin, will bear a child in her old age (vv. 36-7).

This New Testament use of the familiar call to faith of the Old Testament does not end with the infancy narratives (we recognize it again, of course, in the angels' appearance to the shepherds, Luke 2.9-14), but runs through all the Gospels. It is not the language of Paul, though it is clear from Romans 8, 15, that he is familiar with it. The author of the Acts of the Apostles does not hesitate to invoke it for Paul when he is on his way, under arrest, to Rome (ch. 23), and again when, during the voyage, he speaks to the crew as they are in danger of shipwreck (ch. 27). But whenever, in the Gospels, Jesus begins (Matthew 10.26-31, Luke 12.4-7) with 'Do not fear . . .', he clearly refers to the traditional formula. When Jesus comes walking on the water he tells his frightened disciples, 'Take heart, it is I; have no fear' (Mark 6.50, Matthew 14.27). In the case of the storm at sea where Jesus stills the waves (Mark 4.35-41), Jesus draws this formula directly into the orbit of faith: 'Why are you afraid? Have you no faith?' And the motive, as always, is that he is there.

This story from Mark, when it is taken up in Matthew's Gospel (ch. 14, 28-33), contains the added episode of Peter stepping out of the boat to walk on the water himself. But feeling the strength of the wind, he is afraid (v. 30) and calls out to Jesus, 'Lord, save me'. Jesus, reaching out his hand to catch him (v. 31), asks, 'Man of little faith, why did you doubt?'

These Gospel passages use our formula, always the indication that it is the Lord who speaks, as theophanies, showing Jesus as God incarnate. Thus, in Mark 2.1-12, when the paralyzed man is lowered through the roof by his friends, who were unable to get through the crowds at the door, Jesus tells him (v. 5), 'Your sins are forgiven'. The scribes, taking this for blasphemy, ask (v. 6, 'Who can forgive sins but God alone?' Jesus then heals the paralytic 'that you may know that the Son of Man has authority on earth to forgive sins' (v. 10). The terms of our formula are under the surface of Mark's telling of this story, but when it is repeated in Matthew 9.2-7, he adds explicitly the familiar 'take courage' to put it firmly within the orbit of this formula.

Telling the stories of the daughter of Jairus, whom Jesus raises from the dead, and of the woman along the way whose haemorrhage is healed when she touches the fringe of Jesus' garment, all three synoptic evangelists (Mark 5.21-43, Matthew 9.18-26, Luke 8.40-56) use these terms frequently, including the appeal to faith and – a new element, drawn explicitly into the formula – 'Go in peace'.

Many other examples in the New Testament can illustrate the same point: in other miracle stories, at the Transfiguration, in the accounts of the Passion and especially of the Resurrection. When John tells of the risen Christ's appearance to the disciples, he transforms the traditional 'Do not fear', while clearly using the terms we have followed, into 'Peace be with you' (John 20.19 and 21). This is the greeting used, in our liturgy, by a bishop, in place of what a priest would say: 'The Lord be with you'. But what are we to make of all this?

This assurance – 'Do not fear, peace be with you, take courage, the Lord is with you' – whether in Hebrew or in Christian Scripture, makes a central statement of how God reveals himself, and spells out the loving, caring character of his intervention in our human affairs as he asserts his presence. His presence, always supportive, is reason for courage, for faith, not to fear anything that is not he, to be at peace. This is what we mean by faith.[1]

---

1 This entire question of the 'Do not fear' texts in both Hebrew and New Testament Scripture, as basic formula of faith, has occupied this writer for many years. What stands here is an abbreviated treatment of it. I plan soon to publish a fuller account.

Christians and Jews have in common our monotheistic faith, formulated in contrast to the polytheisms of the ancient Canaanite world among which Jewish faith was formed, and of the Graeco-Roman one into which early Christianity was thrust.

There is a fundamental religious sense to those ancient polytheisms. Their basic assertion is that the world we live in is a terrifying place. Their gods and goddesses represented the multiple uncontrolled forces of nature or of human turmoil: rain or drought, the storm, dearth or plenty, war, disruption; forces, personified, that were at best indifferent to us, at worst actively hostile. The task of human life was to hold these hypostasized forces at bay, to protect ourselves and those dear to us from their assaults and jealousies. This made it the work of religion essentially to bribe them, to keep them from harming us, but with the knowledge that ultimately we would lose and they would destroy us. Religious practice was rigorous and demanding, but the world it described was terrifying.[2]

If we look to the faith of our contemporaries, we will find that a great proportion of them believe something very similar to the ancient polytheism. Many go to churches, or to synagogues or mosques, and think of themselves, at least nominally, as Christian, Jewish or Muslim, but their core belief is that the

2 I don't consider this critique of the ancient polytheisms descriptive of contemporary polytheistic religions like Hinduism. Behind the polytheism of Hinduism is a monotheistic current that has to be recognized.

central issues of their lives are to save themselves from loss of their jobs, from harm to themselves or their families, from the house burning down, from war or the many other catastrophes that could befall them.

Some regard themselves as non-religious or post-religious, but in fact this basic orientation of their lives, even without hypostatizing the foes they combat, is a quite religious undertaking; a covert polytheism that identifies the controlling elements of the universe and is centred on protecting themselves, by their own efforts, from the many irrational forces that might otherwise engulf them.

The monotheistic faiths, Jewish, Christian, Muslim,[3] tell us most centrally that none of this is true: that we are not so threatened, that we live in a world that is the creation of one God, can rely totally on his goodness, care, love and promises; that we are safe in his world, whatever comes upon us, and can therefore commit ourselves wholly to his service; and that of all those whom he loves and has made in his image, like ourselves, we can do so without fear.

We will never find this easy. Any of us who think we can get through life without doubts — consider the experience of Mother Teresa of Calcutta — must be paying very little attention to what is happening around us. Flannery O'Connor wrote:

---

3 Regrettably, it is beyond this writer's familiarity with the Qur'an or its language to assess the Scriptural heritage of Islam on this matter in the way we have done with the Hebrew and Christian Scriptures.

'I think there is no suffering greater than what is caused by the doubts of those who want to believe. What people don't realize is how much religion costs. They think faith is a big electric blanket, when of course it is the cross. It is much harder to believe than not to believe'. Our situation, living our faith as well as we can and striving for it, attentive to the voices — all the voices — of our Church, in which we have the leading of the Holy Spirit, is well described in the words of Psalm 26, 7 and 9, which formed the Entrance verse to the Mass of that 11th Week of Ordinary Time in which I started this chapter: 'Lord, hear my voice when I call to you. You are my help; do not cast me off, do not desert me, my Savior God'.

CHAPTER 2

The Theologian's Task:
Fides quaerens intellectum

As the clash of loyalties has developed within the Catholic Church in recent years, suspicions have swirled particularly around the figure of the theologian. We might expect that theologians would be held in respect within the Church, as persons who have dedicated their lives to the exploration of the faith. But those who understand themselves basically as defenders of an embattled faith tend to see danger in the person who asks questions about it rather than simply reciting inherited formulae.

During the late 1980s and early 1990s we had a debate within many of our Catholic institutions of higher learning on whether we wanted a Department of Theology or a Department of Religious Studies. The question presented itself as one of objectivity. Was the work done in these departments to be based on presuppositions of faith or, should it treat such suppositions simply as phenomena, which are to be examined without prior commitment? Because the university is supposed to be the place of dispassionate examination of all claims to truth, it became a struggle for those of us who insisted that our theology be an expression of those suppositions of faith.

Academic integrity would surely suffer if theologians understood their task, as many bishops would have liked to see, merely as apologetics for what the bishops themselves were saying. The faith criterion must be internal to the theologian's work, not just conformity to an external formula. But eventually those of us who saw the faith supposition as integral to theology do seem to have won out.

The task was complicated by new responsibilities that theologians faced in the wake of the Second Vatican Council. First, ecumenical studies, in which we sought to find the community of our faith with other Christians who often enough employed different formulae, disturbed the surface of Catholic uniformity. Then interfaith studies, as the thrust for reconciliation and mutual respect among the different faith communities became a priority for us, raised these questions in a particularly acute way. We have had to recognize that Judaic Studies or Islamic Studies, too, should proceed on suppositions of their faiths as we recruited representatives of other faith traditions to our departments.

Thus the classic definition of theology given by St Augustine in the fifth century and championed by St Anselm in the eleventh, *Fides quaerens intellectum*, 'Faith seeking understanding', comes again to the centre of discussion. The Holy See and the bishops have also got into the act, with the *Ex Corde Ecclesiae* request — not, it should be noted, a demand — that everyone teaching theology in a Catholic institution seek a mandate from the local bishop.[1]

That request caused much panic in theology faculties, as it raised the prospect that the teaching of theology would be subjected to the whim of bishops untrained in the discipline of theology, and whose concept of theology was, at times, indistinguishable from catechetics or the blind defence of the establishment. It fell into very general desuetude as the bishops' own custody of their office came into disrepute with the sexual abuse crisis. Few bishops have continued to raise the matter since their standing with their own public was undermined in that way. However, it lurks in the offing as a potential threat, many theologians feel, to the seriousness of the theological enterprise.

---

1 The initial Apostolic Constitution, *Ex Corde Ecclesiae*, 'On Catholic Universities', was promulgated by Pope John Paul II on 15 August 1990. It went through much discussion and consultation with university presidents and theologians in the Vatican's Congregation for Christian Education until the October 1998 promulgation of an *Ex Corde Eccelsiae* Implementation Document Draft. This was visited thereafter regularly by the United States Conference of Catholic Bishops and the Association of Catholic Colleges and Universities for its application in the United States. The ACCU carries on its website a closely reasoned critique of the document, 'Academic Freedom and the Vatican's *Ex Corde Ecclesiae*', by Daniel C. Maguire, edited for publication from a letter of 25 January 2002, from Maguire to Archbishop Rembert Weakland, O.S.B., of Milwaukee, where Maguire's institution, Marquette University, is located.

AUGUSTINE'S USE OF *FIDES QUAERENS INTELLECTUM*

For Augustine, the question of the process of theology was largely a procedural one. He concerned himself, in many of his writings, with what he saw as the great issues of philosophy, which for him were the study of man and of God. Augustine is even peculiarly ambivalent about the distinction between philosophy and theology. As a rational creature, man was so much made to know and love God that Augustine found it all but impossible for anyone to fail of that knowledge. 'You have made us for yourself and our heart is restless until it rests in you', he writes at the very beginning of his *Confessions* (1,1,1), and he draws the conclusion, in his *Sermon* 69, 2–3, 'There can be found only a few of such impiety that these words of Scripture would be verified of them, "The fool has said in his heart, there is no God." This madness is restricted to a few'.[2]

The line between philosophy and theology thus becomes hard to draw in Augustine. Not only does he see knowledge of God as connatural to man, he even believes that knowledge of both Father and Son should be matters of Natural Theology; though he wavers on whether the work of the Spirit and hence

---

2 I rely here, and in the following remarks, largely on the analysis of Augustine's writings in Ralph McInerny, *A History of Philosophy*, vol. II, Part I, Chapter II, available on the internet from the Jacques Maritain Center at Notre Dame: http://www.nd.edu/Departments/Maritain/etext/hwp202.htm

knowledge of the Trinity can come without revelation. In this, though, he approaches the matter from a very different direction – he is practically at one with Immanuel Kant, for whom knowledge of God had to be fully attainable by natural reason.[3]

Still, our knowledge of God remains, for Augustine, radically imperfect and subject to corruption. The sources of our knowledge are authority or reason. Those less informed, he believes, do best to learn from authority, the better informed through reason. Yet given the obscurity of our natural knowledge of God, we must nevertheless all rely primarily on his revelation of himself, and from that must reason our way to an understanding of what God has revealed. Thus Augustine comes back to reliance on the experience of God revealing himself, and insists that we then use our reason to understand that experience.

---

3 Kant felt obliged to argue that the truth of Christian revelation, which he accepted, had to be equally available to all human persons, as a mark of God's justice. This justice could not discriminate against those who had no access to its historical teachings, hence available through reason alone. Positive revelation, though, was necessary because of the results of human sin. See Immanuel Kant, *Religion within the Limits of Reason Alone*, translation and introduction by Theodore M. Greene, Hoyt H. Hudson and John R. Silver (New York: Harper Torchbooks, 1960). I owe this reference to Roger Haight, S.J., in *Dynamics of Theology* (Maryknoll, N.Y: Orbis Books, 1990), p. 53.

ANSELM, EXPLORATION OF THE MEANING OF OUR FAITH

Anselm, immersed in the writings of Augustine, took Augustine's phrase, '*Fides quaerens intellectum*', as the original title of what he eventually called his *Proslogion* to theology. Because, like Augustine, he is a man of faith, he accepts without any wavering what God has revealed. But because, as man, he is a rational animal, he must also meditate and reflect on what has been proposed for his belief. From this will come such measure of understanding as he attains.

But does one merely start from faith, or is the process so imbued with faith that it is as present at the end of the process as it is at the beginning? Anselm will not claim the authority of faith for his conclusions. Those are efforts, necessary but entirely human efforts, to understand. In the preface to his *Monologion*, he tells us he seeks to base truth not just on Scripture but on argument and the 'necessity of reason', *rationis necessitas*, but that Scripture is the source of every problem he discusses. Faith, which he understands as the acceptance of Scripture as true, is the starting point. Historian Ralph McInerny expresses Anslem's thought so: 'Given faith, one can concern himself dialectically with what he believes. This is why, after the Apostles, the holy Fathers and Doctors have said so much about the content of faith. Their writings are ordered not only to confuting the foolish and correcting the hardness of heart of those who do not have the faith, but also to nourishing those whose hearts are already cleansed by faith and who can take delight in reasoning about their beliefs'.[4]

For ourselves, then, what has this formula, *Fides quaerens intellectum*, to say? It is first of all a matter of whether the theologian begins from a solid supposition of faith or not. It is further a question of how we are to proceed from this initial supposition. The theologian is essentially an inquirer, not simply an expositor. The task calls always for fundamental questioning, not on whether the tradition, the 'deposit of faith', is true or not, but on what it means. This task differs from that of the Magisterium, which is basically expository: determining what items truly and essentially belong to that tradition. A task which one hopes will be exercised with some modesty.

Anselm, like Augustine, requires of the theologian wisdom, moral maturity and reverence for the data of faith, yet he will not claim certainty of faith for the results of his efforts. However, not to explore these matters of faith in quest of understanding would be to default on the theologian's responsibility.

---

4 For Anselm, this rudimentary account also relies on Ralph McInerny, *A History of Philosophy*, Part III, Chapter II, posted on the internet by the Jacques Maritain Center at http://www.nd.edu/Departments/Maritain/etext/hwp210.htm

ASKING THE QUESTION: THREE PHASES

I have been in the habit, for some years, of translating the Augustinian phrase, *fides quaerens intellectum*, rather rudely: 'What are we talking about?' This is the essential question the theologian must pose, and at three distinct phases of our response to revelation. We do so, first, at every stage of the study of Scripture. Beyond that, however, our Church has become very much fixated on doctrinal pronouncements of varying degrees of authority, made by Popes, councils or bishops. These can form no substitute for the authority of Scripture or *The Tradition* of which St Paul speaks (and which precedes New Testament Scripture).

But we have in the history of doctrine a complementary and supplemental tradition. Of this, too, as a second level of the task, the theologian must ask the same question: 'What are we talking about?' And there is a third level at which we must ask the same question. We are men and women living in a specific time that challenges our faith in distinctive ways. We cannot separate ourselves from the circumstances of our own lives, and so must ask our questions of the normative documents of our faith – the Scripture – and of the doctrinal tradition in terms of our actual experience of life, personal and communal, and of revelation as it has been mediated to us. What, in these very concrete terms, are we talking about?

If, beyond this, we recognize that faith is not simply a number of propositions which call for our assent but a way of living in response to the self-revelation of God, our emphasis is going to be much more heavily on the witness character which we find in the Scripture than on the subsequent doctrinal tradition. It is for this reason that we have gone through the lengthy excursus on the 'Do not fear . . . because I am with you' texts, in the last chapter, which have so much to do with the object of our faith. Our faith is in God. He has spoken to his people throughout a history, and has manifested his presence in Christ, assuring us that we can place full trust in him. That is what we live by.

What light will this throw, to take one of the more contentious questions among the various Christian bodies, on sacraments and their efficacy for salvation, and in fact what degree of centrality to faith and life will such a question have? We will address this in a later chapter. Whose teaching would need to be of concern, as a danger, to the Roman Congregation for the Doctrine of the Faith, whose target population consists so much of Catholic theologians, and on what basis? How would theologians relate to such bishops who might have no notion that these were the actual concerns of theology, and who might deny the teaching mandates suggested by *Ex Corde Ecclesiae* on the basis of this ignorance?

And so we arrive at the present state of our Church, where defensive attitudes prevail both on the part of hierarchy, conscious of its status and responsibilities as Magisterium, and on the part of individual theologians and the theological establishment as such. We need a clarification of roles if this relation is not to be one of tense confrontation. It sometimes appears that this confrontation becomes, from either side, an assertion of power rather than of faith. We will come to deal with that, too, in a later chapter, and on the need for reconciliation as an essential dimension of our life of faith. But first we need to consider each of those three phases of the theologian's task in turn.

I. SCRIPTURE

Two events of the twentieth century have enormously eased our theological approach to Scripture, making this now the least contested area of the theologian's task.

It was not always so. At the beginning of the twentieth century, during the campaign against Modernism, Catholic central authority tracked down and disciplined any theologian or scholar who let himself be lured by the historical-critical methods that had come into use in late nineteenth-century Protestant scholarship.[5] Condemnations and teaching bans,

---

5 The campaign began with the issuance of the Encyclical *Pascendi Dominici Gregis* by Pope Pius X on 8 September 1907. This followed the catalog of sixty-five proscribed errors in matters of Scripture and Catholic doctrine, *Lamentabile sane exitu*, a 'Syllabus Condemning the Errors of the Modernists'. This was issued by the Holy Roman and Universal Inquisition, 3 July 1907, and was itself followed by the prescription of the Anti-Modernist Oath on 1 September 1910, to be sworn by all clergy, pastors, confessors, preachers, religious superiors, and professors in philosophical-theological seminaries. The literature on the campaign and the subsequent modifications of the oath is very extensive, but is well summarized in the article 'Catholic Oaths and Academic Freedom',

much like those that have more recently been imposed on Catholic moral theologians, became the order of the day. Restrictive rules were placed on Catholic scholarship, such as the prohibition of vernacular translations other than from the Latin Vulgate. So important a figure as Ronald Knox got caught in that bind, having prepared, from the Vulgate, his very literate English translation of the Bible just before that restriction was lifted.

Pope Pius XII abruptly changed all that with his encyclical, *Divino afflante spirito*, of 1943. Issued on 30 September, the feast of the ancient biblical scholar and Vulgate translator of Scripture himself, St Jerome, this became the *Magna Carta* of Catholic biblical scholarship. Far from desacralizing the text, study in the original languages, critical apparatus, a view of the

---

published by Michael B. Lukens, associate professor of religious studies at St Norbert College in De Pere, Wisconsin, in *The Christian Century*, 1 November 1989. The oath was radically revised in 1967, following the Second Vatican Council, becoming a Profession of Faith, including the Nicaeno-Constantinopolitan Creed and a short-list of principal teachings of the Magisterium but omitting the explicit anti-Modernist strictures. But the stakes were raised again in February 1989, when the then Prefect of the Congregation for the Doctrine of the Faith, Cardinal Ratzinger, added three further sentences with more explicit commitments, concluding: 'What is more, I adhere (*adhaereo*) with religious submission of will and intellect (*religioso voluntatis et intellectus obsequio*) to the teachings which either the Roman pontiff or the college of bishops enunciate when they exercise the authentic Magisterium *even if they proclaim those teachings in an act that is not definitive*' [italics added]. For many theologians, that submission even to non-definitive teachings of the Magisterium, which particularly require investigation, creates a problem.

historicity of the Bible texts and the use of form and historical criteria have opened up the Scriptures to levels of understanding that had simply been closed to us before. Even today you find rear-guard actions, articles posted on the internet to say that Pius XII could not really have meant that, and trying to return Catholic scholarship to about the level of fundamentalist biblical literalism. However the effect of Pius's action has been to reveal the meaning and context of the Scriptures to us in a way that previously had been unattainable.

The second event was the publication on 18 November 1965, by the Fathers of Vatican Council II, of their Dogmatic Constitution, *Dei Verbum*, 'On Divine Revelation'. The date was the anniversary of Pope Leo XIII's 1893 encyclical *Providentissimus Deus*, which had first given some encouragement to the critical study of Scripture by Catholic scholars; an encouragement drastically retracted, first by Pope Pius X's anti-Modernist crusade after 1907, and then in 1920 when Pope Benedict XV, in his forbidding encyclical *Spiritus Paraclitus*, required acceptance of the most literal meaning of every word and verse of Scripture, down to asserting that Moses himself had written every word of the Pentateuch, including Deuteronomy and the account of his own death.

The Council Fathers had been presented, when they first assembled in 1962, with a draft constitution on the (plural) 'Sources of Revelation', reflecting the traditional dichotomy of Scripture and Tradition as two distinct sources of revelation. The churches of the Reformation had challenged that two-source theory, insisting on the *sola Scriptura* principle that became a mantra of Protestantism. In the familiar manual theology of the time, 'tradition' tended to be understood as a special wisdom imparted to the Church's magisterial office, expressed in the doctrinal statements of councils and popes. It was this claim of a doctrinal authority equivalent to that of Scripture that the Reformation churches had rejected, while Catholic teaching had gone on comfortably with the two-source theory until this preliminary draft was rejected by the Council Fathers in 1962.

In their eventual Doctrinal Constitution *Dei Verbum*, debated at length in committee and in the *plenum* of the Council, the Fathers determined that there is in fact only one originative source of Revelation, and that is the action of God himself, revealing himself in his conduct toward his chosen people and in the event of Christ. We have access to this self-revelation of God through tradition; that tradition referred to by St Paul when he tells us (1 Corinthians 11.23): 'For I received from the Lord what I also handed on to you, that the Lord Jesus on the night when he was betrayed took a loaf of bread . . .', or (1 Corinthians 15.3-4) 'For I handed on to you as of first importance what I in turn had received: that Christ died for our sins in accordance with the scriptures, and that he was buried, and that he was raised on the third day in accordance with the scriptures . . .' Paul had commended his Corinthian community because (I Corinthians 11.2) they 'maintain the traditions even as I have delivered them to you'.

Paul writes this, of course, before most of the New Testament Scripture was written. The tradition precedes the Scripture, and the Fathers of the Council, recognizing this, spoke of one source through which we have access to that revelation, rather than two, and it is The Tradition. The Scripture is witness to the tradition. Only in the fourth century would a Canon of New Testament Scripture be agreed, and at that point the criterion was that these books, and not others that were rejected from the Canon, represented the faith of the Christian community, i.e., The Tradition. The books, of course, are very complex, and contain much that is hard to reconcile with much else that is there. But that The Tradition was contained there was not a matter of doubt.

On this basis, we Catholics have discovered in ourselves much more affinity with the '*sola Scriptura*' Protestants, recognizing that in our time these Scriptural books are our one most solid contact with The Tradition. They are therefore the *normative documents* of our faith, the testimony to the Tradition of faith as received by the first Christian generation. To discover, within these normative documents, The Tradition, requires of us that we approach these complex witnesses to faith with all the historical/critical means that we can muster. Hence the question for the theologian of the Bible: What are we talking about? What do these normative documents really say of the Tradition of faith?

II. THE DOCTRINAL TRADITION

Catholic theology has long given enormous weight to the doctrinal definitions generated, in councils or through the teaching of popes and bishops, over the course of the Church's history. I can remember, when I was in my undergraduate theology courses in Germany in the early 1960s, we had our hierarchy of sources, among which, in theory, Scripture ranked higher than the doctrinal tradition. But in practice, when we went to our exams, our basic preparation was to quote the relevant definitions of doctrine, reciting back their numbers in the Denzinger collection. What was '*de fide definita*' was the last word in authority, and these definitions seemed like solid planks nailed firmly in place to form the floor of our Catholic faith.

As our theological institutions have opened up to a more critical assessment of the tradition, the hot-heads among us have inclined to disparage this aggregate of doctrinal positions, to the great alarm of traditionalists who still see the doctrinal tradition as the central core of the faith. These definitions tend to be articulated in far more philosophical language than those normative documents, the Scripture, whose authority is much higher than theirs. They represent the endeavour that has gone on throughout the Church's history to carry out the theological task itself: to ask, within some area of the faith, what are we talking about? At critical times in the experience of the Christian community, these questions have been so acute that the authoritative magisterial level of the Church needed to come together and formulate a response.

It was not the cultural habit of the earliest Aramaic-speaking Christian community, represented in our New Testament Scripture, to look for precise definitions of doctrine in philosophical language. That was instead the genius of the Greeks and of their language. The Greek Fathers set themselves to the task at once, and we in the West carried their tradition over, as well as we could, into Latin, a language considerably less congenial to this process than Greek. You notice that things are getting fuzzier as we carry on our theological discussion in the highly developed modern vernacular languages, with phenomenology, Wittgenstein and a discussion of the meaning of meaning in our philosophical baggage. Who now could stand up for Augustine's certainty that such things as the existence of God were so philosophically evident that none but a fool could miss them?

The doctrinal tradition, then, is more closely allied to theological discourse than to a kerygmatic enunciation of the faith; though at certain critical times representatives of the Magisterium have made pronouncements of special importance. We can best understand that special importance through the concept of the Communion of Saints. We are, as Church, an historical community. We have our faith through a tradition handed on from generation to generation, from parents and teachers, ultimately from the Apostles as first witnesses to the self-revelation of God in Christ. These doctrinal statements constitute the agreed formulae by which the Church has enunciated things which it found critically important to its faith at particular times in its history. To trash them is to dismiss the generations of faithful people, essential members of our Communion of Saints, to whom it was so important to enunciate them with all the clarity they could find. They should always be treasured because of the reverence we carry for those who formulated them, who with us are the Church. But they must also be interpreted, and with care. This is the next task of the theologian: to seek understanding of these statements, to ask again: what are they talking about?

Each of these doctrinal definitions was fashioned in the language of a historical time and place and hence calls for interpretation, at least as much as does the language of Scripture itself. Their authority is less than that of those normative documents, which are therefore of first importance in our interpretation of the doctrinal statements. The definitions were always a response to particular crises of their time, which called for more precise formulation of some point related to faith. The theologian, consequently, must understand the particular circumstances of that time which called for this special consideration, must understand the contention that surrounded them, the habits of language within which they were formulated, and their effect, positive or negative, on the living practice of faith of those who sought to live by them. Far from being solid planks of the floor we stand on, they too are objects in the theological quest. What are they talking about?

And what has their problem to do with us? And this is not yet the end of the theologian's task, for we must still ask our question, both of the Scripture and of the doctrinal tradition, in terms of our actual experience of living the faith as the Church in our own time.

III. OUR PRESENT EXPERIENCE

Here is the third pole in our theologian's quest for understanding of the faith we actually live. Unless we understand how this relates to our own experience of life, we don't have a genuine understanding of that faith.

This can't mean arbitrary adaptation to some modern ethos, to our own whims or convenience. It is our task, as witnesses to the faith in our own time, to be faithful to The Tradition; that basic Tradition of the experience, witnessed by the Apostles, of the self-revelation of God in Christ, which the Scripture itself, our best contact with that Tradition, and all the doctrinal pronouncements of our history, have tried to mediate to us.

But we do live in a particular time, have our own very distinct and ever-developing modes of knowledge, our constantly evolving and growing awareness and understanding of the world about us, and the vast multiplicity of cultures that are now open to us as well as that one that is our own. We have our special experience of the human condition in an era of great cruelties, massacres and wars, and efforts to control the turbulent currents of our time; the creation, and often the neglect, of endeavours to order our world, to protect our environment, to distribute the goods of this world in some equitable way, to establish norms of justice, to express in all the complexity of our world the presence of God in Christ and to live in such a manner that we witness to his caring, his forgiveness, his will for the salvation of us all. If we cannot express our faith in terms of this, not necessarily as propositional formulae but certainly as a way of life, we have no proper understanding of it.

I've tried to present the theologian's task in realistic terms. It must be clear that it is not simply that of a parrot reciting received formulae of the past. The theologian must have reverence for the doctrinal as well as the more foundational tradition. The theologian is bound to be a disturber of outmoded ways, troubling to the *status quo* because he is always raising questions. The theologian who knows his task has to approach it with some humility, aware of how much he has not penetrated, proof against arrogance in his own opinions, open to instruction from the Church and from the whole community of faith in which he lives.

I hope this understanding of the task will give us a window into the nature of orthodoxy, the topic of our next chapter, in a theologian's teaching, as well as a point of view from which to consider the damaging polarization we find presently in our Church. If our theologians are not permitted to ask their troubling questions, we have become an unthinking Church and thus, truly, betrayers of our faith.

CHAPTER 3

Orthodoxy: Fidelity to the Spirit's Leading

In the course of the many years I've spent as an active peace worker, mediating and interpreting in the Northern Irish conflict, I published an article in *The Month*, the English Jesuit journal, in 1977 titled 'Church Structure and Violence in Northern Ireland'. In it I tried to identify what the Northern Irish Protestants were troubled about in Irish Catholicism, and found that the central problem was their perception, rightly or wrongly, that Irish Catholicism was so clerically dominated that Catholic Ireland, they felt, was incapable of democratic life.

Democracy was a matter of such great importance to these Northern Protestants that they identified themselves as a community by it. Their concept of democracy was of a society that preserved, as its most basic value, the rights of dissenting non-conforming minorities, just such as Cromwell had fought for in the seventeenth century. But the dissenting non-conformists in their own society were in fact the Catholics, whom they feared because of this clerical domination. Their failure to live up to their own highest ideals in this matter of the freedom of Catholics was a matter of pain for them, a feeling of guilt so deep that it had to be concealed, and effectively worked out against a scapegoat, the Catholics.

I thought this article would be welcome to my many Protestant friends, as it ought to contribute to understanding and therefore reconciliation between people of the two traditions. But one of them wrote back to me, pleased enough with the analysis, but indignant that I had used the terms 'Catholic' and 'Protestant' as denominational tags. He, as a Presbyterian minister, recited with his congregation every Sunday the Nicaeno-Constantinopolitan Creed, professing faith in the 'One, Holy, Catholic and Apostolic Church'. I should therefore recognize him and his colleagues as Catholic.

Somewhat bemused, I replied that I had no intention of denying him this title in its full literal sense. I recognized him, as one who professed the faith of the universal Church, as catholic in the same sense I sought to be myself. I felt innocent enough in using the terms in a denominational sense, as that was common enough practice. For my own part, I regarded myself as catholic. Since I am not of the far Right, I'm sure there are those who wonder if I am orthodox, but I believe I am, in the sense which I will go on to define here. And as one who is always looking to promote genuine reform in the One,

Holy, Catholic and Apostolic Church, I felt I could claim to be at least as protestant as he was.

WHO IS ORTHODOX?

Our popular concepts of orthodoxy, in an other-than-denominational sense, are likely to be that the orthodox person, teacher, or theologian is the one who has all the answers pat, who gets them directly from pronouncements of the Magisterium and never raises nagging questions. It is according to this concept that the term 'orthodox', and even the term 'theologian' itself, is taken to mean the absolutist, who will brook no question. It becomes comparable to the honourable Muslim term 'Ayatollah'. Its original meaning is the 'image of God', the person so imbued with the sense of God that he images God's justice and compassion. But it has been so abused that it is now understood to mean the irrational dogmatist. That is even one of the common stereotypes that attaches to Jesuits, and to 'Jesuitical thinking'. We Jesuits are supposed to have all the answers, to win all the arguments and know how to put our spin on any subject, if need be at the expense of the truth.

SAVING THE PROPOSITION OF THE OTHER

I would like to look for a moment at a page in the *Spiritual Exercises* of St Ignatius Loyola, a work already familiar to any of you who have ever taken a Jesuit retreat. The page is one that, since I realized what it was saying, I have always hoped might be the most Jesuit thing about myself. It is the *Praesupponendum*, the 'Presupposition' to the Exercises. It reads:

> To assure better cooperation between the one who is giving the Exercises and the one who receives them, and more beneficial results to both, it is necessary to suppose that every good Christian is more ready to save the proposition of another than to condemn it as false. If he is unable to save the proposition, the one who made it should be asked how he understands it, and if he understands it badly, it should be discussed with him with love. If this does not suffice, all appropriate means should be used so that, understanding his proposition rightly, he may save it.

This short paragraph has been put through many processes of translation. The original was in Ignatius's rough local vernacular Spanish. It was rendered into Latin and into a more literary Spanish and eventually into numerous other languages, those more often translated from the Latin or from the more elegant Spanish than from the original. The paragraph scandalized many editors of the *Spiritual Exercises* to such an extent that it was left out of several editions, and when it was retained the final sentence was often translated to mean that the one giving the Exercises should argue the case with the exercitant so as to win the argument and make him abandon his proposition. Not so the original, in which Ignatius is still, even at that stage, arguing that he should be helped to save his proposition, not to abandon it.

You see the radicalism of this procedure. At one time I used to carry it about, copied out by hand in the original rough Spanish, as Ignatius wrote it, in a diary/note-book which I carried about in my pocket. However I ripped out the page to give it to a close associate of the great Lebanese Shi'ite Imam Musa al-Sadr, the Ghandi-like figure who had founded a Movement for the Dispossessed, of all creeds, in Lebanon and was most universal in his dialogue with them all, Christian and Muslim, an ever radical voice of peace. Musa, holy man that he was, had already been 'disappeared' in Colonel Khadafi's Libya by the time I met his associates. He had surely been killed, but his Shi'ite followers in Lebanon, used to the idea of vanishing Imams who would return, sought in every way to plead with Libya for his release. I found that his spirit closely matched what I had learned from the Ignatian *Praesupponendum*.

You note that this is not simply a proposal of Christian charity in our discourse. It is a theory of knowledge, applicable to all, specific to the Christian only insofar as it is a practical living-out, in its openness to the other, of Christian faith. If I am to win all the arguments, know it all beforehand, my mind has already shut down. The 'proposition' of the other, of course, refers to what is truly important in the other's perception, experience or conviction. It is not as if there were no truth criterion. If I am to learn, I must approach the other's 'proposition' with openness. Winning an argument will get me nowhere and I will lose the light that the other's perception could give me. But the other will learn also, coming to an understanding of his own 'proposition' that will enrich it and lead deeper into truth. This is a very different concept, then, of orthodoxy than being equipped with unshakeable certainties at every point.

We have a wonderful example of this Ignatian *Praesupponendum* in the life of the best known of all Jesuits, St Francis Xavier, patron of Christian mission. He had to learn it through life experience. When first sent out, a Jesuit missioned by the Pope himself at the request of the King of Portugal to bring the Gospel to India, Xavier believed that any Indian he failed to baptize was destined for hell fire. He wrote how his arm was tired from pouring the waters of Baptism. He regarded the Hindu priests as agents of Satan. That was until he realized that the people coming to him for Baptism were urged on by the pikes of the Duke of Albuquerque's army.

When Xavier learned that, he was so outraged that he wrote an indignant letter to the King of Portugal, abandoned his position in India, found a ship and sailed off to Japan. Once there, he knew now that he must respect the Buddhist sages and learn from their wisdom, save their proposition as he called on them to respect and save his own. Hearing from the Japanese that they drew their inspiration largely from the Chinese mainland, he set off for China only to die on an offshore island. On his experience his Jesuit brothers built when Matteo Ricci, Ferdinand Verbiest and Adam Schall constructed the Chinese mission in the sixteenth to eighteenth centuries. This was so tragically destroyed when other forces in Rome brought about the condemnation of the Chinese Rites they had fostered; a condemnation retracted in the twentieth century when it was too late. Robert de Nobili's work in India and the establishment of the Paraguay Reductions to protect the integrity and growth of Native American culture were further witnesses to this essential Ignatian spirit of the *Praesupponendum*, never neglecting or contemning the insights of the other person or culture.[1]

RIGHT TEACHING

Where, then, is the criterion of orthodoxy, of right teaching? It is in our openness to the leading of the Spirit. The Spirit, we are promised, will lead us into all truth (John 16.13). Our

---

1 These are extraordinary experiences of Christian mission. Some of the best references for them are *China in Transition, 1517–1911*, Dan J. Li, trans. (New York: Van Nostrand Reinhold Company, 1969); L. J. Gallagher, *China in the Sixteenth Century: The Journals of Matteo Ricci* (New York, Random House, 1953); and Vincent Cronin, *The Wise Man from the West*, (HarperCollins Canada, 1955) and *A Pearl to India: The Life of Roberto de Nobili*, (New York, E.P. Dutton & Co., 1959). For the Paraguay Reductions, the film *The Mission* (1986) is a good introduction.

encounter with the Spirit is in the Church. This is the teaching not only of the Gospel but of the all the ancient creeds, which always associate the Holy Spirit with the Holy Church.

Our first thought in this connection may be of hierarchy and the Magisterium, which are our guides to what is essential to faith. But it is to the whole Church, the entire community of faith, that Christ gives the promise of the Spirit. That puts us right on the fine line people worry about between pronouncements of the Magisterium, at any of its many different levels, and a *sensus fidelium*. I would think that if we had a clear idea of what things constitute the living practice of faith and how much freedom is open to the practicing Christian we would have far less difficulty with this.

The problem will pose itself differently for Catholics simply trying to live their faith and for the professional theologian, basing his enquiry on his faith commitment, though both will approach it genuinely as inquirers. The parish priest is somewhere in between these two: not professional theologian but expected to articulate a *sensus fidei* to his congregation.

Andrew Walls, the Scottish Presbyterian historian of mission, tells a story of the conversion of the Maori tribes of New Zealand that illustrates well the situation of lay people in bringing their faith to realization in life terms.[2] British

---

2 Andrew F. Walls, *The Cross-Cultural Process in Christian History: Studies in the Transmission and Appropriation of Faith* (Maryknoll, New York: Orbis Books, 2001), pp. 20–3.

missionaries, Anglican, Methodist and Catholic, arrived with the British colonial incursion in New Zealand, evangelized the Maori tribes and by 1845 had baptized more than two-thirds of them. The New Testament in Maori had circulated widely, one copy for every two of the population. The Maori, long accustomed to intricate tribal warfare, gladly accepted the white man's religion, because it came with the gift of the white man's ironware, his guns. But the guns escalated the ritualized tribal warfare among them to such a pitch of bloodshed, never before experienced, that the Maori came together to pledge their support for one another and put an end to the warrior aspects of their culture, expressing their new resolve in terms of Gospel teaching. It is at this point, Walls declares, that they became a Christian people. The Maori, he writes, 'responded to the gospel, not to the missionaries' experience of the gospel'.[3]

Most of our people would have quite different practical issues than these to deal with in terms of faith, some deeply personal, some also communal and social. These may be such as the Latin American Base Communities faced, or they might be the endangered culture of marriage in our United States society today. But of course they will also include issues of war and peace considerably more extreme than those that faced the Maori tribesmen.

---

3 Walls, *The Cross-Cultural Process*, p. 23.

AUTHORITY

We have become accustomed to phrase the faithfulness question in terms of whether we have been following orders, which come to us from our political and communal leadership but also, in the Church, from the clergy and the hierarchy. Faithfulness is then judged by whether we conform to the instruction of those above us. We understand well enough the virtue of maintaining order, but a mere unthinking submissiveness is fundamentally foreign to a faith that challenges us to a life commitment. Our relation to hierarchy, one that is properly of affectionate deference, is in fact quite different.

The writings of St Ignatius of Antioch, the second-century martyr–bishop who was carried off to Rome for execution around the year 120, may help us to understand this bonded relation of Christian community to bishop. Travelling by sea in the customary Roman way, the ships timidly hugging the coast instead of sailing across open water, Ignatius visited Christian communities in cities along the way; some of which had bishops, others which had not yet adopted this office of a central monarchical figure, which in fact was quite new in Ignatius's time. His series of letters to these churches are basically in support of this novel episcopal office.

But Ignatius is conscious of the teaching of St Paul, that there is but one mediator between God and man, Jesus Christ (1 Timothy 2.5), one head, Christ our Lord (Ephesians 4.15-16). He must therefore make his teaching on the position of the bishop consistent with that. He accomplishes this through image. Ignatius does not use the metaphor of the bishop speaking in the name of Christ. Rather, he employs a Trinitarian image to depict the relation of the bishop to clergy and people. The image is quite architectural in its depiction of the assembled Church.

The bishop, as was the custom in early centuries, was seated as he addressed the congregation. Were the bishop seen as representing Christ's teaching, he would then be an irrefutable figure of authority. Rather, he represents the Father. Looking out into the congregation, which is standing before him, he recognizes Christ, the Son (Body of Christ). And in the dialogue of love that transpires between them there is the presence of the Holy Spirit.

What the bishop says is the expression of the faith of the community, and has its validation in being that, the faith of the Church. It is through that faith of the Church that all of them together arrive at The Tradition, which is at the root of Scripture. This is thus a consensual concept of the Church's teaching. This Trinitarian image in Ignatius informs the collegial understanding of Church teaching that we typically find in the Eastern churches.

Such a way of perceiving the process of teaching in the Church is represented in later theology by the concept of Reception. What the authority of the Magisterium has pronounced must be received by the Church at large or the exercise has been in vain. This means that in order to know the faith of the Church we must be listening with great sensitivity to what is going on in the Church, what is actually the faith — lived faith — of the full body of the faithful. That is where we will hear the voice of the Spirit. Absolute certainties will be relatively few. The Spirit is leading us to action, not simply to belief in a series of propositions. It may be, of course, that the members of the Church, high or low, are unfaithful to The Tradition and to the Spirit's leading. In that case, we have need of the prophetic voice in the Church, someone who will recognize that and will scream and holler, recalling the membership of the Church to its faith.

All of this brings us to the question: is it possible for a person to be in programmatic error and yet orthodox in his faith and teaching? I certainly hope so, because no person is always right about everything. Hence, if we cannot be orthodox in our faith while in some error, none of us is orthodox. What makes the difference between orthodoxy and non-orthodoxy is then our openness, our readiness to be corrected and not to believe we are unalterably right in our perception of the faith. It is our openness to the voice of the Spirit leading us to all truth within the living faith of the Church. This includes our receptivity to the teaching of the Magisterium, but extends also to our close listening to what is occurring within the community of faith.

DOCTRINE

We have to deal, then, with the history of doctrine in the Church. We touched upon this already in the last chapter.

Doctrine is the result of the Church having asked itself the basic theological question about matters of its faith: what are we really talking about? We do that in our faithfulness to The Tradition witnessed by the normative documents of our Scripture, and in our reverence for the teaching found in the doctrinal history of the Church. That history is represented by the collection of doctrinal statements, differing in their level of authority, that have come down to us, from councils and the teachings of Popes and bishops. It is vital to our integrity as the historical community of faith that we accept these statements of our predecessor generations in the faith, from whom we have received the tradition. To reject or trash their statements of the faith is to reject the people themselves of those earlier generations, discarding them from our Communion of Saints.

We can make a first broad distinction between the polemical and the catholic – I use a small c – pronouncements of this tradition. In every Council until Vatican Council II it was customary to follow up each positive doctrinal statement with a list of the Canons. These were statements in opposition to what the Council had determined, and each such statement took the form: 'If anyone says – such and such, e.g., that the faith is all a nonsense – *anathema sit*: let him be condemned'. As polemical formulae, these statements tended to be sharpened to such

57

an extent that they went to the brink of heresy themselves in order to condemn an opposite error. Most often, those anathematized would respond, whether immediately or at some later time, that this polemical formulation was not truly what they said or meant. This had to lead to further dialogue. And so we have to say, as a generalization, of these polemical statements in the doctrinal tradition that we need to know both sides of the argument before we can properly understand them. This is the work we see going on in the dialogues among churches, bilateral and multilateral, that continue to this day in the search for our common roots of faith.

More important to us are those doctrinal pronouncements which we can recognize as fully catholic (small c still), in the sense that those who formulated them reached out to all the many resources available to them in an effort to frame an accurate statement of the faith of the Church. Among these are the definitional statements that are so precious to us and which especially call for our assent. But of these, too, we must ask the question: what are they talking about? They are all propositional statements made in the past. The language of their framing, generally the philosophical language of their time, which will differ from the language of the Scripture and also from the philosophical language of our own time, has to be understood in its origins and in its context. We need to know why the topic of the statement was a problem to those who dealt with it, how the problem arose, and how important it was to them. And finally, we need to know whether this is truly a problem for ourselves and how we are to deal with it in our own time.

Let me take some examples of such catholic statements of doctrine. A prime example is the Creed, crafted at Nicaea in 325, modified and amplified at the First Council of Constantinople in 381. It was understood as excluding Arian heresy, and was to that extent polemical. But in its positive statement it has served the Church well, a banner statement of the essentials of belief that now carries the assent of nearly all the churches that understand themselves as Christian. Over the extensive period in which Arianism threatened to prevail, and had the backing of emperors and a great proportion of the bishops (who even tried to spin the terms of the Creed to fit their Arian suppositions) this statement of belief stood as a hedge against falsification and eventually succeeded in defining the orthodox faith of the Church.

Another good example is the Decree on Justification of the Council of Trent. The Fathers of the Council went all lengths to plumb the controverted question of justification by faith or justification by works, drawing on all the Christian tradition they could muster. At the time, the Protestant Reformers made an assumption that this would be merely a polemical attack on themselves, and they largely ignored the Decree for that reason. It was not until the twentieth century that the great Reformed theologian Karl Barth read closely into the Decree and found that it was a truly catholic statement, a formula of definition acceptable both to Protestants and Catholics. Barth's student Hans Küng made this essential agreement in faith the subject of his doctoral dissertation, published under the title *Justification*.[4] In more recent years, we have seen formal bilateral acknowledgements of agreement on this doctrine between Lutheran and Catholic churches.

A third such catholic statement of doctrine, one that will concern us in a later chapter, is the Eucharistic definition of the Third Lateran Council of 1215. Here the Fathers defined the relation of the bread and wine of the offering and the Body and Blood of Christ using the term 'transubstantiation'.

This was new language to the Western European Christians of its time, the Aristotelian language of substance and accidents, never heard in the Scriptural accounts of the Eucharist. It had been lost to philosophical usage over many centuries, but brought back into Western currency through Arabic discussion of Aristotle in Spain, and brought to the attention of European Christian philosophers and theologians in the twelfth century through Latin translations of the great Arab philosophers made by Spanish Jews; a remarkable dialogue of religious faith in itself.

The problem addressed by the 1215 Council was one of corruption of Eucharistic faith by an extreme objectifying

---

4 Hans Küng, *Justification: The Doctrine of Karl Barth and a Catholic Reflection*, translated from the German by Thomas Collins, Edmund E. Tolk and David Grouskou (London, New York, Toronto: Thomas Nelson & Sons, 1964), with an introduction by Karl Barth.

interpretation of the words of institution that threatened to reduce the Eucharist to superstition. The Council's formula was designed to prevent that. Three hundred years later, however, the Protestant Reformers professed to see this term, transubstantiation, used to express the very superstition it had been designed to prevent. The Protestants consequently refused to employ the term. The Council of Trent asserted its accuracy and, in true polemical fashion, its necessity, and anathematized anyone who refused to use it.

We can, with due interpretative care, understand and assent to exactly what the Third Lateran Council meant by this term when it employed it in 1215. We can discern just as well the tragedy of mutual misunderstanding that brought about the anathemas of the Council of Trent, and assent to its teaching. But Aristotelian philosophical language is no longer the underlying currency of our discourse. We have read many other philosophers, and the language of transubstantiation may well not answer all of our current questions.

In the last chapter, I wrote of the task of the theologian as necessarily raising such questions as these. Not to raise them indicates, in fact, a lack of that openness to the leading of the Spirit which is the essence of orthodoxy itself. An enterprise that does not make a claim to infallibility for the theologian's conclusions understands that it may be in programmatic error, however much it strives for the truth to which the Spirit leads the Church, but remains open nonetheless to the corrective voice of the Spirit heard in the faith of the Church. The certainties in which we deal are the realm of the Magisterium and need to be stated with some modesty, recognizing the imperfection of our human perception as we strive to live in truth. Our orthodoxy will therefore always be such a striving, and not an imperious demand for conformity.

CHAPTER 4

Polarization in the Church: Quest for Power

The faith questions we face in the contemporary Catholic Church, here in America and elsewhere, have brought out an ugly side of our characters: an inclination to classify other Catholics as the enemy, disloyal to the faith. It all reminds us of the way we Catholics and the Protestants used to treat one another, for the four centuries before we got to Vatican Council II, as merely contemptible pretenders to Christianity. We got over that, but appear to have transferred it now to Catholics who think differently than ourselves.

DELEGITIMIZING ONE ANOTHER

I've been calling this a kind of guerrilla warfare within the Church. We need only look to the efforts, in many dioceses, to delegitimize any of the new autonomous organizations of clergy or lay people that arose in the strenuous atmosphere of the years following the sex-abuse scandal of 2002 — such as priests' forums and the Voice of the People. Much of the hierarchy decided they should pay no attention to voices that spoke without their prior permission. The priests and lay people in these organizations, normally those most interested in the Church and devoted to its teaching, concluded that the bishops who would not listen to them were abusing their authority.

This happened while the whole Establishment felt itself under siege over the sex-abuse crisis, but much genuine good will on the part of the people, who have always been the backbone of the Church, was given the back of the hand. Eventually some of these same scorned organizations fell into a reciprocal striving to sabotage the hierarchical structures of the Church, even by such means as crippling their fund-raising campaigns. The atmosphere of enmity got very ugly.

I live in Boston, epicentre of the sexual abuse scandal that broke with such fury on the American Catholic Church in January 2002. As a result, habits of restraint have probably broken down more here, than elsewhere. Vilification of those associated with the scandal has reached a very shrill pitch, but it has spilled over into the contempt expressed over other issues. When the Boston Archdiocese was faced with the closing of many parishes and the sale of other properties, largely because of the expense of reparations for the sex scandal, what was called the 'reconfiguration' of the Archdiocese, people aimed screams of betrayal at the new Archbishop and all those associated with him. Others suspected of more liberal doctrinal positions were read out of the church in the fiercest terms by those opposed to them, and they themselves were no less vehement in their dismissal of those in whom they see only unthinking conformists.

Such becomes the tone of our discourse. As I first drafted this chapter I included some instances of this extreme language from either side, but I found it simply too embarrassing to quote things whose attribution would be clear enough and which, I would hope, could only shame those who had said them.

What, in the Gospels, has Jesus to say of such indulgence in resentment? In Luke 9.49-50, we hear how 'John answered: "Master, we saw a man casting out demons in your name, and we forbade him, because he does not follow with us." But Jesus said to him, "Do not forbid him; for he that is not against you is for you."' Similarly, in the Mark 9.39-40 parallel: 'John said to him, "Teacher, we saw a man casting out demons in your name, and we forbade him, because he was not following us." But Jesus said, "Do not forbid him; for no one who does a mighty work in my name will be able soon after to speak evil of me. For he that is not against us is for us . . ."' There is some counterpoint in Matthew 12.30: 'He who is not with me is against me, and he who does not gather with me scatters', but the original point is not lost, and what constitutes this scattering does require some definition.

VARIANT OBJECTS OF FAITH

Where, then, do we actually put our faith? This question has engaged us from the start of this book. We have been emphasizing that our faith is not merely assent to propositions. We accept the authority of human persons within the institutional structure precisely because and to the extent that they, in their faith, embody the faith of the Christian communion, which is Body of Christ. We put our faith in God, who promises us his guiding and saving presence, of which Christ is the manifestation. It is in him that we have our hope, on him that we can place our trust. We can live secure through loving confidence in him and live our lives, consequently, in service to him and to the others in whom, he tells us, we encounter him. The many propositions of our doctrinal tradition have their relevance inasmuch as they follow from this faith in God, and need always to be examined to see how they relate to it.

We saw already, in the first chapter, how the peoples of that ancient world, from which our monotheistic faiths sprung, believed that their world was a place of terror. Their many gods were menaces to them or at best simply uncaring of them, reasons for fear rather than confident faith, personifications of the forces, in nature and society, most dangerous to them. Their response, actually a religious response, was to conclude that propitiating these forces was the central issue in their lives, and they devoted themselves to sacrifices and worship to shield themselves, their families and loved ones, from the harm these gods might do. Religious practice was rigorous and demanding, but the world it described was terrifying.

Though our Abrahamic monotheistic faiths all tell us that this is untrue – but that instead we are creatures of a loving God in whose hands we are truly safe – the core belief of many of our contemporaries closely parallels the ancient polytheisms. Many go to churches, or to synagogues or mosques, and think of themselves, at least nominally, as Christian, Jewish or Muslim, but the central issues of their lives are to save themselves from loss of their jobs, from harm to themselves or their families, from the house burning down, from war or the many other catastrophes that could befall them. Any of us seeing the dreadful things that happen in our world is tempted always to understand it in that fashion. We don't, in our day, hypostasize these forces, but if this is our outlook we live a covert polytheism.

Such a religion is common to many, even of our most educated people. But another alternative to confident faith in one God, even more widespread, is a dualism that conceives the world as the arena of combat between the good and the evil, and sees religion as a process of discerning and destroying the enemy. This is the actual religion of those who are ever wary of what they see about them, devoted to loyalty tests and putting their faith in some symbol of authority that can marshal their energies against the darkness.

They, too, may be regular churchgoers, regarding themselves as Christian, or perhaps Jewish or Muslim, but their true faith is in positing themselves, and their ideological associates, as good, against the evil powers of the world, in a warfare which will determine the world's fate. We see much of this in our national discourse in recent years. It is Manichaean, or dualistic in some other form.

And here we encounter the polarization that has come to prevail so much within our Catholic Church: a dualism that seeks to empower itself by the defeat of an enemy. The drive for power over others, rather than any faith in the one God, fundamentally characterizes it, and it consequently seeks its certainties from some other source. What will make the world, or the Church, or ourselves safe? For those who accept this way of understanding their world, it is the power of policing, the capacity to repress dissenting opinion or any action that fails to meet loyalty standards, the solidification of authority in some human agency of control. We can treat the authority system of the holy Church itself in this way, and then we have created for ourselves an alternative object of faith.

Indifferentism has become one of the fashions of our times; the attitude that all religions are 'all right', that there is no value distinction to be made among them. Respect for the religious convictions of others has rightly acquired the character of virtue among us, and I have argued for it myself in presenting the *Praesupponendum* of the Jesuit *Spiritual Exercises* in the previous chapter. This should not blind us, though, to the underlying suppositions of religious outlooks that may be actually harmful. Few of us nowadays will worship at the shrines of Mars or

Minerva or their colleagues in the classical pantheon. But the virtual polytheism of those who see the world merely as a series of perils, and whose only ultimate values are to save, by their own careful action, themselves and those they love from the multiple sources of possible harm that threaten to engulf us, subverts any trusting faith in God who is one, who loves and has saved us, and that whether or not their culture includes going to church. Likewise, the dualism that conceives the world as a battleground juxtaposing good and evil forces, and casts our life as a struggle for conquest over malevolent opponents, is the one thing that will render religion itself evil and a danger to others.

ABSOLUTISM AND COERCION

When we find ourselves convinced that we are the sole possessors of all truth, called to oppose all those who will not accept it, then we have become that menace to the peace of the world. Religion has acquired a very bad name in the world, often seen and more often suspected of being the source and fomenter of violence. If we have to deal with violent conflicts, we find it a task to realize that lives of faith can actually lead to peace and reconciliation rather than exclusion.

Our religious Right has become very sensitive to the charge of fundamentalism. The then Cardinal Ratzinger, responsible for the defence of doctrinal orthodoxy as head of the

Congregation for the Doctrine of the Faith, reacted indignantly to the aspersion of fundamentalism in the sermon he gave for the opening of the Conclave that elected him Pope Benedict XVI. We should not throw that term around casually, but since the suspicion is already in the air we should examine what really constitutes fundamentalism.

It has three most basic elements.

First, it is the effort by a religious elite to impose religious observance on the rest of society. We see this in many forms among different religions. The original usage of the term was to describe the attempt of a certain brand of Protestantism in the United States to demand a biblical literalism in the teaching in the schools. Faithful or not to the spirit of scripture as their interpretation might be (the Catholic Church was making much the same demands of its theologians at the time), what made it fundamentalist was the requirement that the public conform to their understanding. We could see this in the Scopes 'monkey' trial, when a teacher was brought before the court on the charge of teaching Darwinian evolution. Other religions may have a different set of external observances which they require of the public. It may be beards, or head coverings, or conformity to certain core beliefs, such as the divine assignment to a race or faith group of exclusive rights in a land, whether Israeli religious settlers in the West Bank or Hindus in regions of India. Catholic fundamentalism in our own time, we may observe, is likelier to focus on the region of doctrine than of scriptural literalism.

A second characteristic is reductionism. There are, as a practical matter, only so many external observances that can be imposed on a general public. Otherwise they become unenforceable. Here we find the origin of the 'wedge' issue, the selective criterion by which we can judge who are the right and who are the wrong people. In our American Catholic world we hear often of 'cafeteria' Catholics, supposedly those who do not accept the entirety of Catholic teaching. And yet, in their zeal to identify who should be ruled out of the Church for their failure to pass the loyalty tests, the accusers are at least as selective in their own choice of issues. They surely omit from their menu the basic Christian requirements of forgiveness and reconciliation.

The third characteristic is that the fundamentalist demand is essentially an assertion of power. Its criteria have to do not with faith, but basically with control. The worst possible response to fundamentalism, when we recognize it, is to aim for a seizure of that same power over the others, a response in kind that is as fundamentalist as what it opposes.

As I say, let's not throw accusations of fundamentalism around carelessly, but let's also be observant of what is happening. If indeed we are encountering such a selective grasp for excessive doctrinal control by the elite leadership of our Church, we need above all to avoid making a counter-thrust for power, to pull power away from the hierarchy and claim it for local groups. This is equally without any Christian foundation, and we need to do better. We encounter, in either camp, a groundswell of criticism from the others, who believe they act in good faith. Our best response is to presuppose that good faith on their part, and enter into genuine dialogue.

WEDGE ISSUES

We are dealing, in this muddled atmosphere of enmity and presumptions of bad faith, with matters of major moral importance, among which two basic strands stand out. One is the right to life, with its centre on the question of abortion. It has many tentacles, such as the popular temptations of embryonic stem cell research and the parallel questions of assisted suicide and 'mercy' killing. That 'mercy', we may understand, easily slips over into compulsion and pressure on the elderly and seriously ill to get out of the way of the material interests of the young and healthy. It can make our hospitals and the whole medical system unsafe for the inconveniently ill. We tend to treat these issues as absolutes on which we can brook no compromise. But other tentacles of the life question, since they cannot easily be classified as such absolutes — war and the astonishingly casual acceptance of 'collateral' damage and killing of the innocent it entails, death penalties, damages to the environment that endanger the life sphere itself, or consignment by our negligence and selfishness of vast populations to short, brutish lives of deprivation and disease — are treated as nugatory and hardly worthy of attention by the Catholic community.

That item of damage to the environment that endangers the life sphere itself deserves special attention. Those Catholics for whom there is no other question but abortion point readily to the staggering numbers of unborn lives stamped out — a common reckoning is 47 million since the Supreme Court decision of 1973. Beside that, any attack on human life short of World War II seems petty. But consider the global warming prospect of a significant rise in sea levels. In our heavily populated world, we can reckon that Florida and the Netherlands will be no more. That will involve great suffering and loss, but on the part of people who can somehow get away. What of Bangladesh? That, too, will be under water, but here are vast numbers of people (reckoned between 142 and 157 million) who will have no way to escape. Such an enormous toll may well have been made inevitable by the policies of an American administration that deliberately obfuscated these dangers through the years for the sake of profit in the oil industry. Can we write that off as unimportant by comparison with abortion?

The other major matter that engages us is marriage, also tremendously important and seriously threatened. The sexual orientation question has cut across this concern and taken centre stage in American Catholic attention. We have learned something about not discriminating against persons of homosexual orientation; the rest of the world has by now convinced us that 'homophobia' is a mortal secular sin. But our Catholic authorities have defined the phenomenon of calling same-sex unions 'marriages' as the major threat to the institution of marriage in our time. Surely it is not that, but a para-phenomenon that hardly impinges on marriage between the sexes at all.

The true threat to marriage, foundational institution of society that it is, is the common lack of commitment to the good of the other as much as to our own, and the consequent prevalence of divorce. Our culture, and evidently our Church, has failed to foster the capacity for fidelity. A shocking proportion of marriages, as much among Catholics as among any others, are casually dissolved, partners discarded, children abandoned to a life of disruption, treated as pawns in the battles of their parents. We hear far less of this than of 'gay marriages' from those who want public enforcement of their moral agenda. True and loving commitment to the good of another becomes extremely difficult for our own young people of marriage age to achieve, for lack of serious attention to building, within the Church, a culture of such self-giving, of forgiveness and readiness to sacrifice for the good of the partner and the children. Surely, in such a situation, the nearly exclusive concentration we see on the 'wedge' issues is a shamefully profane indulgence.

In both these areas, the life issues – at least the 'absolute' ones – and the defence of marriage against the 'gays', we have put the burden almost entirely on Catholic politicians. Other Catholics will be treated with hatred if they do not toe the line on these topics, and in this way a reactive 'Catholic Left' is called into being, which acts as if these questions were not truly of importance. But the Catholic politicians can effectively be punished by rallying an angry bloc of Catholic voters against them and making their election to office impossible.

A choice has been made here by those who adopt this tactic. They have decided to act on their legitimate convictions about the importance of the issue of life by trying to compel acceptance as a matter of obedience. They would like to exclude the expression of an opposite opinion from the public square. They want to elect officials who will legislate their convictions, or will choose judges, at various levels up to that of the Supreme Court, who will prohibit violations of the life ethic, whether at the level of abortion or that of embryonic stem cell research or the end-of-life issues. The choice is to do this as an act of power over the public life of society.

But they do not have the power to accomplish their mission, or to exclude those other voices from the public square. Their opponents happen to own the public square. They are not able to elect officials who would or could actually carry out their program. Public opinion in the country, ill-informed though it be, ensures that such a program, even if put into law, would simply be defied, and on too wide a scale to control. All those espousing this kind of program are really able to do is to exclude any Catholic candidates who recognize these obvious facts from public life, or have any influence in the body politic. Blindness to the political reality is then taken as the only legitimation for a Catholic candidate.

All this was evident during the election campaign of 2008. It came to a level of confrontation during the annual November conference of the United States bishops just after that election, when bishops with the bit between their teeth challenged the representative of the Holy See, which had clearly determined not to go to war with the new American administration over that issue to the neglect of all else. And we then had the spectacle of protest at the invitation of the newly inaugurated President Obama, sign of so much hope to so many people at home and abroad, to the graduation at the University of Notre Dame. It would be difficult not to conclude that the issue of abortion was, in this case, not nearly so much the centre of the protesters' concern as was the obedience of Catholic public figures and institutions to the Catholic bishops.

Let's not minimize the importance of the life issues involved here. They are clearly, as many of us see, integral to a Catholic or Christian outlook on life, and can be equally clear to people of other religious faiths or none who reverence the dignity of all human life. But, in fact, they are not clear to a significant majority of our fellow citizens. Those opposed to us on the life issues actually believe that they are doing good, defending the rights and dignity of others, whether women or the terminally ill. That means they require from us persuasion, and a witness that consists in our commitment to the whole life agenda, including those things that are not 'absolutes'. They are not suitable matter for acts of power, especially of a power we don't really have. How well are we doing at this persuasion?

It has been my own custom for several years now to hold, in the chapel of our Jesuit residence at Boston College, St Mary's

Hall, a Mass for Life on (or near) the 25th of each month from Annunciation Day in March until Christmas, a period representing the gestation of the child Jesus in his mother's womb. We pray for the safety of unborn children in danger of abortion, and those who place no reliance on prayer may well smile at the notion. Many of those who assemble for these Masses are convinced that the only way to work for this cause is to try to elect public officials who will ban abortion. My own message is that we have a responsibility to lay hold of the high ground, becoming the defenders of human life in all the ways it is threatened, allying this cause clearly to the advancement of the human.

The late Cardinal Joseph Bernardin presented this cause eloquently, calling it the 'seamless garment', a 'consistent ethic of life'. It is very noticeable that these life issues have been associated, by many of their advocates, with the far political Right, those who on all the other ('non-absolute') life issues — war, death penalties, torture and excessive punishments, indifference to illness, suffering or oppression — take the anti-life and anti-human positions. Even when it comes to the partisan politics of an electoral campaign we see the advocates of a pro-life power position condemning candidates of the more liberal party (especially if they are Catholic), but not rejecting equally pro-abortion candidates of the more conservative party. Such behaviour not only cannot be successful, but it discredits the pro-life credentials of its advocates as well, as they associate their cause of the defence of life with those who are really opponents of life issues in every other area. Notre Dame was a sorry spectacle, but the murder of an abortionist doctor did more actual damage to the pro-life cause than anything else we could imagine.

We need not be over-impressed by the politicians, Catholic and other, who profess to be personally opposed but unwilling to impose their belief on others. For some this is true, for others simply a convenient ploy. But we should be no better impressed by those for whom the defence of helpless human life is merely a wedge issue for the gaining of power. This is not an exclusively religious issue, but a matter of human rights, even in their most secular form. We will not win the argument by association with those to whom human rights are of no real importance, but only by giving witness of our own real commitment to human rights on all scores and convincing the public that the dignity of all life is an integral part of that cause. I could put this more directly by saying we will never win the life argument from the Right, only from the Left.

PARALLELS TO OTHER ERAS

We Catholics, along with others, have in some earlier instances suffered an ethical blindness: a failure to recognize where essential human rights have been most threatened and where there has been a stubborn defence of the worst abuses. The blindness has come from our politics, not our religious faith. The issue of slavery in the nineteenth century provides a conspicuous example where general Catholic opinion and the teaching of our bishops refused, right through the Civil War period, to recognize wrong in the 'peculiar institution'. We had plenty of company in this blindness, of course. The importance of the issue was enormous. We might note that even the effort, through a civil war, to force compliance with a more humane standard did not succeed in bringing about respect for the full human dignity of the African Americans who had been so unjustly kidnapped and enslaved. Instead it took nearly a century before we even began to address the issue of their civil rights. As late as the 1950s and 1960s the efforts of a Fr Louis Twomey, S.J., with his periodical publication from Loyola University in New Orleans of *Christ's Blueprint for the South*, were regarded as needless troublemaking in much of the American Catholic world. By now we realize that we have learned some new things about basic ethical life in this area, and our earlier attitudes are an embarrassment to us.

Equally shaming as a fundamental moral blindness in our society (in no way limited to Catholics who nevertheless shared the general refusal to see that anything was wrong) has been our attitude to women and their rights, a blindness that goes right back through our recorded history. Pioneers of women's equality have had to struggle fiercely all through the twentieth century against entrenched attitudes to bring this issue to the prominence it holds today. Wilful blindness about it remains commonplace. Those of us who strive to educate our own attitudes on the subject have to realize that much of what we say or write now, in our still benighted state, will read as highly embarrassing in another century when people have learned to deal intelligently with women's rights.

I would argue a parallel between these two instances of blindness to the rights and dignity of others and the acceptance of abortion in our current society. Overcoming that blindness will require a change of heart throughout our society. To some extent, we can see it happening already. The building blocks for it will be a growing public awareness of the actual humanity of the unborn, things that scientific research is now increasingly showing in a way that gets through to our public conscious-ness, and the witness of a consistent ethic of life that does not brook the dehumanization of any others. The abortion issue, as an issue of human rights, stands in a contentious relation to another issue of human rights — that of victimized women. If we are serious about life, and about human rights, we have to deal with this conundrum.

HATRED AND DIVISION

How have we come to the pass that such issues as these provoke such angry hatred and division among Catholics and across the whole of our society? The divide antedates these particular matters of contention. The very use of these matters as wedge issues reveals the power-struggle basis of our enmities.

I write this chapter around the time of the Jewish feast of *Tisha B'Av*, the annual commemoration of the destruction of both the first and second Temples in Jerusalem. Rabbinic tradition says that the first Temple was destroyed because the people were not keeping the laws. When the second Temple was destroyed, however, the people were scrupulously observant. But observance was not enough. The Temple was destroyed, the rabbis tell us, because of *sinat hinam*, causeless hatred among the people.[1]

Christian faith prescribes, in fact, another way of dealing with such matters. It is the way of dialogue and reconciliation, working to the assumption that the other is speaking in good faith, even when our disagreement is most grave. Particularly within our Church, we need to learn again how to address each other civilly, to examine our differences with love, to recognize one another's dignity, mindful that in one another, even when we most trouble each other, we are encountering Christ. The true meaning of our lives (Matthew 25.31-46) will emerge from how we treated him in that encounter.

Our Catholic Church, in the United States and perhaps much more widely, suffers from low morale just now. Clergy and lay people alike seem discouraged and to have low expectations of the Church's influence, in their own lives or in the public realm. Business-as-usual in embattled dioceses, reeling

---

1   Observed by Rabbi Malka Drucker, of the Rabbinic Cabinet, in a note for *Tisha B'Av*, 12 August 2005, http://www.malkadrucker.com/

from the blows of scandal and division, has degenerated into a preoccupation with institutional management. This pre-occupation deals a death-blow to enthusiasm for the faith and its work. The kinds of questions we have dealt with in this chapter have been allowed to fall into this groove, the principal concern being how Church leadership can prove that it is on top of these situations, commandeering the assent, even if reluctant, of its discouraged and disillusioned faithful. Those whose hopes for the Church rest basically with reasserting the power of hierarchy become indignant at the spectacle of this low morale among others, and believe that they have abandoned the faith. When risks are taken, or counter-cultural positions asserted, it often appears that such institutional power objectives as these lie behind them, and our efforts are then seen by others as fundamentally corrupt. Participation in the worship and sacramental life of the Church wanes drasti-cally, and applications to priesthood and religious life become so few that we are threatened with a Eucharist-less Church.

The holding back of young people from the idea of religious vocation which so characterizes the state of our Church is often attributed to the celibacy rule for priests, with a supposition that relaxing the rule to allow for the ordination of married men would cure the problem. I really doubt that. Perhaps it is important that optional celibacy for priests be considered seri-ously by the leaders of the Church, who seem to be whistling in the dark when they plead for generosity while refusing to attend to such questions. But the true malaise in this matter of vocations, just as in the lassitude of an often believing Catholic public about Sunday Mass attendance, will yield rather to the sight of the Church doing good things; serving that whole humanity which God has created with such love in ways that are informed and intelligible, and not infected with the self-serving smell of institutional maintenance or business as usual.

CHAPTER 5

Facing the Sex-abuse Crisis: Call for a Council of the Church[1]

The revelations of the clerical abuse of children that burst so rudely on the American Catholic Church in a *Boston Globe* article of 6 January 2002, and mushrooming explosively since, have tremendously exacerbated the angers and divisions that already existed among us beforehand. By now, more than seven years later, many among us would like to believe that the worst is past and that we can now put it all behind us, 'move on' as they say. Others of us believe that is too shortsighted, and that the crisis unleashed in 2002 remains latent in all our disturbed relations within the Church.

---

1 This chapter is a development of an article published earlier, in *Human Development*, Summer 2003, under the title 'Task for the Next Church Council', and subsequently reprinted in the Boston College publication, *The Church in the 21st Century*, Fall, 2004.

I would see the crisis as of Reformation size. It touches the fundamentals of order and authority in the Church. If, as in the upheaval of the sixteenth century, our response to it is basically defensive, it will produce division among Christian believers as lasting and deep as that caused by the Reformation itself, with the difference that this time many will simply abandon religious practice altogether.

The traditional, and Christian, response to such crisis in the Church is to talk to one another, and the full way that is done is through an Ecumenical Council.

Have we a new Council of the Church in our near future? A lot of people, especially those who would most likely be called to account in a Council, have great fear of it. When Pope John XXIII determined on holding a Council back in 1959 the rather sclerotic Catholic Church of the time faced a broadening crisis of relevancy, but nothing like the catastrophe we have experienced since January 2002. As we discovered how widespread was this crisis of the sexual abuse of children by priests, how long a time it had been going on and how church leaders had disastrously failed to deal with it, we entered a devastating period of collapsing trust and fierce recrimination.

STUMBLING RESPONSE

The bishops of the United States, meeting in Dallas in an atmosphere of near panic in June of that year, placed some new obstacles in the way of actual abuse by priests. Whether they found the effective cure or not still remains to be seen. Their formula for dealing with past abuses struck many as posing serious doubts about due process, thereby raising a new controversy of its own. But when, in that November, they tamely accepted its drastic revision by Roman authority, people feared that any crackdown had been essentially compromised, that American bishops had now abdicated responsibility for meeting the crisis, leaving it up to curial officials in Rome. Those officials, in turn, failed to command trust, as they appeared anxious to sweep everything under the rug. Discussion of the Christian imperatives of reconciliation and forgiveness, after Dallas, faded out of the picture. The Church's leadership appeared too distracted even to consult its own tradition, and responded, for the most part, only to the insistent media pressures.

We had urgent questions about whether the bishops, whose actions horrified us even more than those of the pederast priests, would be held accountable in any credible way. That was terribly disillusioning for all who wished to have confidence in the Church as an institutional structure through which to live their faith. Accountability, the ultimate red-line question for the Roman authorities, constitutes a quite distinct issue from the pervasive sexual disorders. Since the time the Cardinal Archbishop of Boston had to resign his see, calls for other resignations abounded, all referred to the Pope as the only one who could judge, order or accept them. Roman officials shrank from the thought, fearing that bishops might go down like a row of dominoes.

An outstanding piece of research done by reporters for the *Dallas Morning News* (published 12 June 2002, for the edification of the bishops then meeting in the city) established a claim that some two-thirds of the bishops of dioceses in the United States (at least 111 of what they classified as the nation's 178 'mainstream', or Roman rite, Catholic dioceses) had in some way protected or concealed offender priests, brothers or other religious. *New York Times* reporter Laurie Goodstein, writing 1 December 2002, widened that count, claiming such offence in all but two of those dioceses. All this told us how far such a purge might go. Many angry people would have loved to see that happen. However, if we were to attack the problem root and branch, we had to be clear that its roots were in Rome, from where the policy was enforced that protection of the institution's reputation from scandal took priority over nearly anything else.

That was not to say that the Pope did it. This is the sort of thing that comes from a bureaucracy. Nor should we be surprised. This is the way of large institutions, as examples ranging from Enron to the United States Government constantly teach us. Bishops, most of them too timid even to criticize, simply followed institutional procedures. We had to suspect that a bishop who would not go along, who refused to place the avoidance of scandal at the top of his list, would have lost his job.

We have serious questions, then, to ask about basic habits in the Church. Angry though people may be, we make fools of ourselves if we believe that a few hangings, a reign of terror in the Church, will resolve these issues. Our ills are so endemic to the system that it is mere evasion to heap all the blame on individuals. Venting our outrage on them may give us some self-indulgent satisfaction, but does not address the underlying problems at all.

Two obvious questions stand out: one about our attitudes toward sexuality, the other about the governance of the Church. On both matters our whole process needs to be opened up. And while there may be other ways of doing this, that is the traditional task of a Council of the Church.

It was a tragedy that the crisis should occur in the waning days of the dynamic Pope John Paul II and cast its shadow over his time. These issues were already of long standing before he began his long pontificate, and very likely effectively concealed, even from him. We don't yet even know with any certainty if these problems arose or were exacerbated by the 'sexual revolution' of the 1960s or whether they go much further back in the Church's history. Many would feel that, for all his extraordinary accomplishments and the love with which he was surrounded, Pope John Paul's penchant for concentrating authority intensely at the institutional centre, while he himself was occupied with other matters, threw a great deal more power than normal to the Curia. This institutional centre had any bureaucracy's distaste for hearing bad news and inclination to cover it up.

Now we have a new pontificate, with Pope Benedict XVI apparently intent on reform of the Curia, and no one knows it or its habits better than he. Whether or not the cardinals who elected him recognized that this was the task he would face, it is on him that the burden now rests of addressing this Church catastrophe in an appropriate way.

THE SEX-ABUSE QUESTION

Anyone can see the social immaturity, especially the retarded psycho-sexual development, of the predator priests we have heard about. There have to be reasons for that; things in their experience and formation that have led them to these perversions. We hear a good deal about sexual sin, but basic attitudes toward sexuality are one of those things that we shy away from discussing in our Church.

It is not to our credit if we regard one of God's most precious gifts to us with the disdain and evasion that human sexuality has received in much of our tradition, the furtiveness with which it is treated. This applies not only to Catholics but to most other Christians as well. The anti-sexual tradition goes back to St Augustine, who is so attractive to Protestants, to many of his contemporaries and even older authorities. It actually has its roots in the pagan world of their time, its dualism (reflected in the Manichaeism that had so attracted Augustine) and its disgust with the body and the material circumstances of life. We can see it as much in Protestant Puritanism as in Catholicism.

In the recruitment of our Catholic clergy and religious, this creates the opportunity for young persons simply to evade or postpone dealing with the issue of sexuality at all, treating it as something that has nothing to do with them. Surely we know celibates who, even much later in life, have never genuinely faced themselves. This is especially tempting to those with some ambivalence, uncertainty or fear about their own sexuality. We may try to screen out such persons as candidates, but can expect little success if the screeners themselves share those attitudes.

The bishops at the Second Vatican Council made a concerted effort never to accept this disparagement of the sexual character of human beings and the sexual expression of human love. The defence of celibacy in their Decree on the Life and Ministry of Priests, *Presbyterorum Ordinis*,[2] was careful never to go near this demeaning outlook on sexuality. But the poisoning tradition still holds on; one that sees persons' sexuality as the bad thing about them of which they should be ashamed, and try to live as if they didn't have it. Discussion of this whole area has long been treated with such reluctance and suspicion as to contribute to a widespread immaturity in our community. So much so that we ought not be surprised when it leads to bizarre consequences like this priest-paedophilia or ephebophilia. The wild chaos of sexual permissiveness that characterizes so much

---

2 *Presbyterorum Ordinis*, 7 December 1965, Chapter III, 'The Life of Priests', Section 2, 'Special Spiritual Requirements in the Life of a Priest', No. 16.

of our contemporary scene can actually be seen as simply the reverse side of this same coin.

Many commentators, some with pre-conceived agendas, want to approach this pathology with instant solutions, like the abolition of mandatory celibacy or the ordination of women, without going through the more fundamental reflection that the matter requires. These issues will doubtless come into the picture and eventually have the attention of such a Council as we may hope to see. (They did come up at the last Council, Vatican II, but were taken off the table and reserved instead for curial consideration.) But we owe it to the integrity of the faith to examine this void in our understanding of the human person more carefully before settling for easy solutions.

Many, even among those of manifest good will toward the Church and its traditions, question whether celibacy or virginity can ever be other than damaging to the persons committed to them. No one will be able to defend their value convincingly unless a mature and welcoming understanding of sexuality and sexual identity become common property of Christians. We can be grateful that the present Holy Father, Pope Benedict, has more seriously addressed this question than practically any previous magisterial document in the Church in his encyclical letter of January 2006, *Deus caritas est*, but we still need a full conciliar treatment of it.

Even more pressing, however, is the question of authority structures in the Church.

THE AUTHORITY QUESTION

We have seen protection of the institution and its managers set above even the most basic moral responsibilities. Our foundational Christian Scripture calls for the most open dealings among us. The 'rulers of the gentiles', we are told, 'lord it over them, and their great men know how to make their authority felt', but 'it shall not be so among you' (Matthew 20.25). Ours is to be a Church where 'there is nothing hidden, but it must be disclosed, nothing kept secret except to be brought to light' (Mark 4.22). To appeal to such fundamentals of Christ's teaching sounds simply ironic today, and we need to ask why.

We have become a very law-bound Church. That in itself accords ill with the priorities set in the letters of St Paul, where we learn that our salvation is by faith, and not by the works of the law. We search our Scripture for a 'Law of Christ', and what we find, in such places as the Sermon on the Mount, is instead an insistence that we must never satisfy ourselves with observing merely the requirements set by a law. Instead we must always strive to do more, to put ourselves at the service of others: never by constraint, but by willing offering of self. You can't codify that.

That makes the Christian community an unwelcoming place in which to develop a legalist culture. We have a different kind of mandate from Christ, more difficult perhaps, but freer. The Christian community is to build up its members in a living of the faith, the confident service of God in others around us, especially those most in need. Limitation to a prescriptive law is not its foundation. But of course, the Christian community eventually became large and complex, acquired respectability and a great deal of secular responsibility for civil society, first under Constantine and his successor emperors and again in the harsher eleventh century. By then it found itself in need of orderly structures for its own governance.

What happened was that it turned, for lack of any specifically Christian structure of law, to purely secular sources. Just by reason of time and place, the Christians who established our institutional canons of law adopted the categories of Roman Law, which still dominate not only the Canon Law of the Catholic Church but also, as Code Napoleon, the legal systems of most European countries.

That law is Roman but has no essentially Christian character to it. It is the law of empire, and its governing premise is that the will of the sovereign is law. That this should have become the basis of Canon Law is entirely anomalous. It is the very system of domination that Christ so explicitly rejects for his followers. It has provided a kind of order, essentially an imposition of order, to much of Europe ever since Roman imperial times, but it has as its fundamental flaw that there is no room in it for the accountability of those who govern to those whom they govern.

By no choice of his, but by the simple fact of his rank within this system of Roman Law, a figure such as Cardinal Law in Boston, like any other bishop, caught though he was in the headlights of a condition that is fundamentally commonplace throughout the Church, was constituted judge of his accusers. How could he escape this? Early in the debacle, his diocesans attempted to construct an association of the existing parish councils, bodies of the most devoted of all his Catholic people: a much milder venture than the better-known Voice of the Faithful. The inevitable response, in terms of the law as constituted, was to reject the association as something built other than on the executive's will, hence potentially divisive. Much later in the fateful year 2002, shortly before his resignation, he did finally agree to meet Voice of the Faithful representatives, but his initial observation to them was that he wished they had sought his permission before forming their association. The Cardinal was accountable, not by his own choice but by the situation common to all his fellow bishops, only to higher authority. Calls for accountability from below could only be an anomaly.

Is this form of legal structure of the nature of Christianity? By no means. Christianity, as Chesterton once told us, has not been tried and failed. Instead it was found difficult and never tried.

We are often told that the Church is no democracy, and the reasoning has been, essentially, that this Roman imperial system is the form of its law. But that has nothing whatever to do with Christian principle. It was adopted only because it was the most obvious law available at the time when the Church first found itself so extensive an institution as to need some such structure of order. It has had so long a tenure in the Church's experience that it will be a painfully intricate thing to extract ourselves from its tentacles, should we so choose, but that is the enterprise that our current predicament demands. It will demand a longer commitment than the duration of a Council of the Church, but its initiation is properly the work of a Council.

Doubtless many of the authority figures who reign in the Church would find it much more comfortable to resist any accountability. They've lived without it as long as they've had their jobs. But the situation has now become untenable. The executive chair in the Church-as-corporation has been standing empty. This posed a constant dilemma for the late Pope, although a centralizing figure, was much occupied with his many travels and writings, with the result that so much was left to curial offices. Yet he also asked earnestly for the thoughts of all Christians on how his office might better contribute to unity in the Church. This has got to emerge as a main topic of discussion as our Church reflects now on the crises it faces. For the present Pope Benedict XVI this has to rank as one of the top items on his plate.

Alternative structures of law, as models for order in our enormous Church, are hard to come by, and we can hardly expect that a system of order faithfully Christian in its inspiration will come easily or quickly. We are much attached, in the United States, to the Common Law system of justice that we inherited from English experience. Common Law, built on the binding force of precedent, does produce accountability, rendering the rulers as responsible to the law as are the subjects. It has constructed a thick planting of the land with precedent laws that bind the ruler as well as the subject, and thus protect the individual from the arbitrary will of authority. So much, so good! It has been the seedbed of as much democracy as we have yet attained. But it, too, has its dark side, in its massively adversarial and vindictive character. Our American culture has become savagely punitive and vengeful under its aegis, as witness, among other things, its attachment to the death penalty or its urge to take away from those imprisoned — proportionately more prisoners than in any other country — anything that can be taken away. It can make no more claim to be proper to Christian life than can the Roman model.

What remains? There are, of course, multiple systems of law we could draw on, many of which are free of either the arbitrary, unaccountable character of the Roman Law or the exclusively retributive character of the Common Law. Many of these systems of justice exist among peoples whom we in the West tend to look at patronizingly, as having civilizations less complex than ours. Yet South Africans, seeking a more wholesome system of justice than they received from the European colonists, have found much of value in the native African concepts of *ubuntu*.

Lawyers and judges in our country, and in some parts of Europe and Australia, have experimented with systems of Restorative Justice, in which the objective is the restoration of relations in society rather than mere retribution, but these remain a novelty, still in their teething stage. Those so inclined have found some useful lessons in the practices of American Indians, the circle-sentencing concept among their most attractive features. None of these, though helpful, have specifically the inspiration of Christian Gospel behind them, but then neither has our current Roman-Law-inspired law of the Church.

Are we capable, then, of constructing a system of internal order for our Church that would genuinely spring from sources within the Christian Gospel tradition? The process would have to begin by recognizing the profoundly a-Christian and even anti-Christian character of the law we presently have; disruptive of Christian living, corrosive (as we are seeing in the sex scandal) of the most fundamental values of Christian faith. We would have to reflect long and carefully to build an ordered Church community that truly related to values of that faith, and could not expect to construct it at one stroke. We have a time before us to learn some of the humility that is so conspicuously lacking in the system by which we now operate.

The Second Vatican Council, in fact, went some distance toward constructing such a system in the first two chapters of *Lumen Gentium*, the Dogmatic Constitution on the Church, but they have since been negated, first by a distrustful period of anxiety, and then by a concentrated period of clawing back from any tendencies toward the accountability of those who govern.

AN ECUMENICAL COUNCIL

Is this indeed the work of a Council? We may well believe so, and one much needed in the face of the deservedly low esteem into which the governance of the Church has fallen. The Council would need to face squarely both of these outstanding questions: the sexuality question and that of law and structure. On the sexuality question the Church needs to hear from many persons of authority, intellectual and spiritual, other than bishops. Just as much, on the matter of law and a structure of service, humility and accountability, many others apart from the bishops of the Church need to be heard and respectfully consulted.

The crisis of the sexual abuse of minors by priests is not merely a Bostonian or an American problem but an Irish, a French, an Austrian, an Australian, a Canadian, a Polish, an Italian and, universally, a Church problem. After smouldering so long and only recently exploding in our faces after lengthy concealment, it has made these questions so acute that they can hardly be evaded any longer.

We face challenges to the basic credibility of our Church, and hence of our teaching, on no less a scale than those of the sixteenth century. The Catholic Church responded poorly then, and paid with centuries of division and dissension among Christian believers when its mere defensiveness turned the attempted Reformation into a lasting breach. If we should treat the present crisis as less serious than it is, we can expect to see disruption of a comparable sort.

CHAPTER 6

Practice of Faith, Expressed in Word and Sacrament

There is an ecumenical element to what we have been saying about faith. We try, as Church, to live our faith, not merely assent to propositions. But there are others who set their lives by this compass of Christian faith as well.

We Catholics had the habit, over several centuries following the Reformation, of regarding Christians of the Protestant traditions as only questionably Christian, as the 'heretics', whom we could leave out of our concept of the Church. Most of our people didn't know much about the Orthodox, but reserved the term 'schismatics' for them, an expression that was much fuzzier in most Catholic minds. They, of course, were just as rude to ourselves.

All that changed, to the amazement of most of our people, with Vatican Council II, when representatives of all these other Christian traditions showed up as invited 'observers', honoured, their opinions sought and carefully considered, and we reflected on whether to call them 'churches' or 'ecclesial communities'. Councils, since the eleventh-century East-West schism, had represented only the Western Church. The Orthodox churches of the East, for that reason, had questioned their ecumenicity. At Vatican II, with all churches present or at least welcome, that situation was improved. The others still had no vote, but they were consulted and their voices were clearly heard and respected.

And now we are back again to standing far apart, ignoring one another except in a few little enclaves where ecumenism is still spoken of. Especially for the angrier parts of our several constituencies, differences of a single-issue character tend to convince us that the others are not really Christians like ourselves. We have great need of seeking each other out, understanding in what ways we share with one another faith in Christ, and exploring, one with another, how we can let that sharing grow. Are we indeed fellows in our Christian faith, or are we entitled to regard one another's faith and credentials as Christians as fundamentally deficient?

I take part regularly in giving seminar courses offered within our consortium of nine theology schools in the Boston area, Catholic, Protestant and Orthodox, all at the Boston Theological Institute. Since the consortium is not a further academic institution on its own, we offer them under the auspices of different schools each year.

The first time the venue was the Greek Orthodox school in

our group where we found ourselves told in the first session, quite clearly, by one of the Orthodox professors that there is one true Church and they are it. Finding both my Protestant and my Catholic students nonplussed at this, I observed that this language had been just as familiar in the Catholic Church as well, but that we had tended to back away from it since, during Vatican Council II, we became aware of the pitfalls of a triumphalist view of the Church. The Church is not identical with the Kingdom. What we are promised is more, unimaginably more, than what we see.

Everything about our Church is provisional, a foretaste and prophecy of what is to come. The most splendid of our art and architecture will fall to dust. Our Scripture, our sacraments, our hierarchical order are all provisional only, awaiting the fulfilment of promises in the *eschaton*. Our faith is something we strive for; hoping always that the Lord will lead us deeper into the mystery of himself and his presence. Hence we must look on ourselves and on our credentials as people of faith with some humility, and recognize that the others striving for this, are also fellow Christians.

WORD AND SACRAMENT

We go to church on Sunday. Some of us — and some of them — go far more often than that, and some, more than others, try to live the rest of their lives in accord with what our churches signify.

What are we looking for there? Clearly, union with Christ; and if we are at least moderately well instructed, we seek communion with one another in Christ, the Communion of Saints which is Body of Christ. That is what Protestants are seeking as much as we Catholics. The Orthodox are perhaps more conscious than either of us that their communion is in the Spirit.

For Protestants, the principal way of achieving this communion is the Word. Their service is constructed so. Their hymns are a form of prayer, not, as in our Catholic churches, processional music to accompany the celebrant priest's entrance or exit, or the congregation's procession to communion. They will sing all the verses, reckoning that the whole text is integral to the hymn. The prayers and Scripture readings must truly speak to them, and hence be carefully presented, and if the Pastor's sermon fails to stir them to a better realization of the Christian life or otherwise meet their expectations, they will get rid of him.

In times past, most Protestants were wary of sacramental liturgy. They had felt, in Reformation times, that Catholic liturgy had reduced the Eucharist to superstition, and were reluctant to celebrate a Communion Service more than once or twice a year, or at best once every other month, even though Calvin had wanted it every Sunday and Wesley had wanted it every day. It was then, in many churches, a hurried early-morning service, held without preaching for a very few communicants, before people came to church for the main service, with the sermon. But over the course of the twentieth century many Protestant churches, even some of Zwinglian heritage, became more interested in the sacramental life, whose importance had always lurked in the background of their consciousness, affirmed always in the terms of Luther's recognition of both Word and Sacrament as the essential marks of the Church.

Eucharistic prayers, truncated at the time of the Reformation, began to be elaborated in terms very familiar to Catholics. The frequency and popularity of Communion Services grew steadily, at different paces in different denominations. In Anglican or Episcopal churches the celebration was seen, once again, as the Mass, and the celebrant as priest, and it became normal that the sacramental action should follow upon the sermon. Yet, for all that, the thing that Protestants saw as uniting them with Christ was still the Word. If the sacramental part of the service was well done and spoke to them, that was fine, but it was an extra, a bonus.

Catholics go to Mass. That is our Sunday — and other — celebration and our way of being united in communion with Christ. We are united with one another, too, in Christ, if we happen to think of it, even though many of our people are still habituated never to talk in church, even consciously to exclude attention to those around them.

We have been accustomed to a lot of rather shoddy presentations of the Mass. This disappoints us gravely, but with our *ex opere operato* theology we have put up with that. The Mass does its work, and Christ is present, even if it is miserably done. Of course, there are many who have become fed up with that, and no longer attend.

People used to be afraid to go to communion, but now they practically all come, and participation in the dialogue of the service is general, even if, in our own country, our people cannot be got to sing. If the Mass is well presented, if the sermon actually speaks to people's hearts, that is very welcome, even a great joy to the congregation, but it is an extra, a bonus. The essential thing is that they went to Mass, and in that way were united with Christ.

I speak of this often in my classes at Boston College, and find that my students are intrigued to recognize it. Once aware of this dichotomy of expectations — Protestants from the Word and Catholics from the Sacrament — they intensely want both, as is quite right and proper, and the natural (super-natural) order of the liturgy.

But what of the Communion Service, the Eucharistic celebration in the Lutheran, the Presbyterian, the Methodist, the Anglican or Episcopal church? Or in other churches? What really happens? Is Christ present? Does he absent himself, not accepting their liturgy? Are these churches sacramentally rejected by God?

We Catholics do not recognize the validity of their celebration. We are likely to regard it as a nothing, as an empty ritual, to the great distress of our Protestant brothers and sisters in Christ. We have argued this along two lines. One is that they do not have ordination in the line of Apostolic Succession, and hence their ministers have no competence to celebrate the sacrament. Many Anglican clergy have so internalized that

Catholic argument that they have sought validating ordination from Eastern or Old Catholic bishops. The other argument is that their understanding of the Eucharist itself is inadequate or reductionist. The September 2000 document, *Dominus Jesus*, of the Congregation for the Doctrine of the Faith, the then-Cardinal Ratzinger's dicastery, refused the name 'church' to any body of Christians that lacked, in this way, Eucharist or a ministry in Apostolic Succession. Recently we have had this outlook repeated again, in less peremptory form, in a set of questions and answers about the Church from that same Congregation.[1]

That might be the end of the question. But the expression itself, 'validity' or 'invalidity', spurs some hope that the question may not be altogether closed, and we ought to understand its meaning. Much, but not all, of this may be a matter of whether, in examining the evidence, we actually want to find either a positive or a negative answer.

VALIDITY

Validity is a term of law. Things are valid which are recognized by an authorized legal authority. We can see this in the case

---

1 Congregation for the Doctrine of the Faith, *Declaration 'Dominus Jesus', on the Unicity and Salvific Universality of Jesus Christ and the Church*, 6 August 2000, especially No. 17. From the same Congregation, *Responses to Some Questions Regarding Some Aspects of the Doctrine on the Church*, 10 July 2007.

of a valid passport or driver's licence. The Department of State recognizes me as an American citizen when it issues me a passport. The Registry Office of the Commonwealth of Massachusetts believes I am competent to drive a car when it issues me a licence. Both authorities are going to take care not to issue these documents if I am not what I claim to be, but we all know that there are not only forged licences and passports but that we can actually deceive the authorities into issuing us documents which they regard as valid and legally acceptable. For all the effort to make such legally recognized documents available only to those really entitled to them, these authorities are not gifted with infallibility.

In the Catholic Church, we take great care for the validity of marriages and baptisms. There is an Ordinary Minister of baptism, who is the Pastor. He has to delegate his authority to an assistant priest, or the priest uncle or friend of the family, to administer the baptism in his place. A record will be kept, which will be consulted when the person wants to marry or be ordained, or seeks another sacrament. We accept baptisms conferred in other churches (if convinced that they have done it properly: a validity question of which, for our purposes, our Catholic authorities are the judge) or by the nurse in the hospital, and will duly record that fact in our register, making exception to the regulation that the baptism must be done or delegated by the Ordinary Minister.

The validity of a marriage comes under question only when the couple wishes to break apart. The marriage must have followed our elaborate regulations to be recognized as valid in the first place. When it breaks up, as happens now so frequently, people go through a still more elaborate judicial process before an ecclesiastical marriage court to see if there were some defect that rendered the marriage null from the start. Very often some such defect is found, and we can recognize a value in the procedure of seeking a declaration of nullity in that it helps the partners in failed marriages to understand what, perhaps from that first moment, was wrong. On that basis, Church authorities will declare the marriage invalid, though they had regarded it as valid until then.

All of this is far less than a certain science. If some defect can so often be found in the marriage that went wrong, what about the marriages that succeeded? It must certainly happen, given the culture of our time, that partners have entered into marriages with some mental reservation – we'll try this and see if it works out – or some settled determination – there will be no children from this marriage – that would in fact qualify the marriage for a declaration of nullity if one were ever sought. But if in fact the couple live happily ever after and, despite their initial reluctance, raise a family, what should we say? Is that a real marriage or is it not? 'Real', in this case, is exactly the quality that those who judge its validity sought to determine. Or take the case, surely not uncommon, in which the evidence brought before the marriage court, and the parade of witnesses, spins the case to make the annulment come through. The court has then been deceived, and an actual divorce given in a marriage that, in its inception, had the genuine consent of the parties. This may even all have happened in good faith, as the parties simply strove, without much understanding, to make the best of a bad situation.

This, then, is a quite uncertain process. It illustrates how the questions of validity and reality, much as we seek to make them overlap to the point of identity, may not be so.

ORDINATION BY A BISHOP

In the matter of the competence of Protestant ministers to celebrate Eucharist, we have required, as the criterion for ordination by a bishop in the line of Apostolic Succession, a bishop ordained by a bishop ordained by one whose ordination goes back to the apostles themselves. A difficulty exists here, inasmuch as the office of bishop, in the form we know it as a central monarchical figure with sacramental and doctrinal competence in a jurisdiction, does not appear in the early Church until the time of St Ignatius of Antioch, about A.D. 120. Ignatius himself is certainly a bishop in our sense and, as he travels, under guard, from city to city on his way to a martyr's death in Rome, he encounters churches that have bishops and others – among them, interestingly, Rome – that do not.[2]

---

2 Among many excellent studies of this late development of the office of bishop, I would recommend the book by Fr Francis D. Sullivan, S.J., *From*

The office of bishop, appearing commonly but not universally around the Eastern Mediterranean in Ignatius's time, did become common, though still not universal, in the Western areas — in Italy, Spain, Gaul or North Africa — before the middle of the second Christian century. Most scholarly authorities would not see anyone certainly exercising the centralized authority of a bishop in Rome before Pope Victor I (189–97). What of the intervening period between the Apostles and the development of this office of bishop?

We can study the evidence that, in the period of the New Testament writing and Apostolic Fathers, there was a variety of church orders, a gradual development toward uniformity in these matters, and that the Christian communities had no great difficulty in accepting this. This chapter is no place to argue this through in detail, but the question is the object of serious study by Protestant and Catholic scholars and appears to be quite open.

What of Apostolic Succession in that case? Surely Eucharist was constantly celebrated all through this time as the characteristic liturgical action of Christians, but the question of who would, as we would put it, say Mass or perform other sacramental rites hardly arises in the documents of this early period. Concepts of faithfulness to the tradition and Apostolic Succession appear to refer much more to teaching than to ritual, even as successive or parallel forms of office and authority develop. Surely people

---

Apostles to Bishops (Westminster, Maryland, Newman Press, 2001), p. xxx.

knew the answers to such questions in their own communities. There was church order, even if, in the small communities of the Pauline churches, it could be very simple and rudimentary. But there appears to have been variety in it, and a process of development and convergence. Given all of this, a matter of history, we could conclude (*ab esse ad posse*) that the developed form of church order that we have received from antiquity is not the only way that Order can exist in the Christian Church.

And yet, from some time in the latter part of the second century, the Church, East and West, has had an Episcopal-Presbyteral Order which we Catholics and the Orthodox preserve to this day, and which was unchallenged until the time of the sixteenth-century Reformation. There is clearly danger in what we have been saying — that we might conclude that Church Order,[3] or a particular Church Order, does not matter, that we are free to experiment with regard to forms of order as we please, and that the defenders of the established order have tied their careers and authority to a false premise. Such a conclusion would have catastrophic effect, producing a kind of confusion that would disrupt the whole mission of the Church.

And mission is vital here. For the Church to act as Body of Christ, Communion of Saints, active witness by a community of faith to the presence and action of Christ in the world, it

---

3 We might note that we use the term 'Order' in two ways in all this discussion: as the structured institutional form of the Church and as the sacramental Order to which deacons, priests and bishops are ordained.

needs to be recognizable, visible. And that visibility is built very largely upon Church Order. One has to know where and what the Church is. We are not speaking here of the Reformation-period argument about the visibility or invisibility of the Church, but of visibility as a condition of its mission. We cannot make this an absolute, but it is a constituent of prime importance for that visibility.

SEPARATED BODIES

What happens, then, when a considerable body of Church finds itself separated, in good faith, from the normal sources of order? We can cite two instances.

In Japan of the seventeenth century, the Edo regime successfully exterminated the entire Catholic clergy, priests and bishops. The country then went into a period of excluding itself entirely from the outside world that we have since described as the Closed Door Policy. Japan's Catholics, finding themselves without a clergy to celebrate Eucharist, with no one to ordain priests and no prospect of getting them, continued to baptize their children and say their prayers, but lived their faith without benefit of those sacraments that depended on an ordained clergy. They continued so until, in 1853, United States Navy Commodore Matthew C. Perry arrived with his 'black ships', and the closed door was opened to, among others, a new missionary Catholic clergy.

The Reformation Protestants of Europe had already made a different choice. Separated from the sources of Order of the Catholic Church, in their case by their own action, and out of a suspicion of its practices and rejection of its authority, they sought a way to replace the existing Order with new practices of their own. They attempted to design them on the model of the New Testament churches which, as we have seen, preceded the Episcopal-Presbyteral Order that had obtained for so long and remained the standard of Catholic and Orthodox practice.

EXTRAORDINARY SITUATIONS

Was this legitimate? It has its traditional theological basis in the principle that in the absence of ordinary ministry, in the extraordinary situation, *ecclesia supplet*, the Church provides. The Church, in this case, for lack of a recognized hierarchy, was understood as the community, Body of Christ, Communion of Saints.

It is on the basis of this *ecclesia supplet* that we have the Extraordinary Ministers of baptism: the nurse in the hospital or any person who can baptize in a life emergency. Canon Law has, as one of its principal tasks, to specify the Ordinary Minister of each sacrament, and it tries, so far as it can predict, to provide an Extraordinary Minister for any case (the extraordinary situation) in which the Ordinary Minister cannot be had. Our two-millennium Catholic history in fact provides numerous incidents of officially recognized extraordinary ministry, even instances involving ordination and Eucharist. But the truly extraordinary situation is the one that was not foreseen.

GOOD FAITH

The essential condition of this is that the action is taken in good faith, *bona fide*. We can cite instances in which this good faith is demonstrated by going to the juridical authorities, typically to popes, for authorization, but this option was not available in the circumstances of the Reformation.

For some four centuries and more after the Reformation, we Catholics and the Protestants screamed execrations at each other and presupposed, on either side, that the other was acting in bad faith. That entailed the supposition, again for both sides, that the other was not truly Church. And if the other is non-church, acting in bad faith, the result of its actions can only be anti-church, anti-ministry, anti-sacrament.

In our own time we have withdrawn that supposition of bad faith. As a general realization of the actual Christianity of these other communities grew upon us in the twentieth century, we Catholics, at least since Vatican Council II, have accepted in principle that the other churches can be presumed to be in good faith, and not only the churches as they are now, but also the Reformation generation that broke with our Catholic communion for reasons that they believed in good faith. There may be exceptions, of course, such as people acting out of spite or some other discreditable motive, among them or among ourselves as well, but the fundamental assumption holds.

RIGHT FAITH

What, then, of the argument that the Reformation churches adopted reductionist views of both ministry and sacrament that nullified the essential character of either or both? Here the question is of right faith, or orthodoxy, much as we examined it above in Chapter 3.

And it is here that we theologians must acknowledge the authority of Magisterium in the Catholic Church. The churches of the Reformation contended sharply with us over the meaning of Order and Eucharist. None of them, as we acknowledge in according them the assumption of good faith, set out to reject the tradition that had come from Christ through the Apostles with regard to any part of the faith, including the sacraments. Judgment on these disputes, or any such re-examination as I propose here, belongs within our Catholic discipline to the Catholic Magisterium. What any theologian believes will not confer validity on the ordination of a Protestant minister or the Eucharist celebrated in a Protestant congregation. A theologian can only raise a question of the reality of that ministry or that sacrament, and suggest reasons to the Magisterium for a reassessment of their juridical opinion on the sacramental reality of what is done in Protestant churches. This exercise would have to be done separately for each church and for each different conception of the meaning and reality of these rites, and it is for this purpose that our churches have been conducting discussion in bilateral and multilateral commissions ever since the time of Vatican Council II.

The validity question, as mentioned above, belongs, for us Catholics, to our Catholic magisterial authorities. Members of another church, of course, will refer this juridical question of validity to their own authorities. They will call on the Anglican Church, by its own internal mechanisms, to rule on the validity — their belief in the reality — of Anglican Orders or Eucharist. Lutheran, Presbyterian or other churches will also rely on their own internal order to rule on their own internal concerns. For them, and for our own Catholic Magisterium as well, the ultimate criterion will be the Apostolic Tradition itself, the faith tradition to which our common Scriptures are witness, and we Catholics are as much subject to the authority of that Tradition as anyone else.

HOW SHALL ALL BE MADE ONE?

Through much of the history of our Christian separations, both the eleventh-century breach with the Eastern churches and the sixteenth-century Reformation break-up, we have assumed our own total rightness, and the sole fault — i.e., bad faith — is with the others. Our model of the unity of Christians was that all the others should acknowledge their fault, repudiate those practices in which they differed from us and return to the embrace of ourselves as the one true Church. We have sought this by individual conversions of Protestants. In the case of the Eastern churches, we have encouraged breakaway units to separate themselves from their parent churches to reunite with us. The Holy Spirit, we have supposed, leading the Church into all truth, has been with us only, never with them.

This model of 'The Return' no longer obtains with us. These other forms of the communion of Christians, even if they arose initially, as I have suggested above, as instances of extraordinary ministry, have since then been the institutional setting within which people of Christian faith have learned that faith and passed on the tradition. Hence they have become the ordinary ministry for those who received the faith in their settings. Are we to suppose that the Holy Spirit has been simply absent to all these developments? Rather, we should suppose that, with the disappearance of any of these forms through which the tradition of authentic Christian faith has been handed down, the whole of Christianity would be impoverished.

The task of the unity of Christians, then, and the model for their unity becomes the exploration of one another's faith understanding, the search for and the nurturing of community in faith — saving the proposition, as we described it in Chapter 3. This is a work of dialogue. It is not of irenicism, ignoring genuine difference or misunderstanding in the transmission of that original Tradition, but always of examination of ourselves as well as them.

I have concentrated, in this chapter, especially on the sacramental dimension of the divisions among Christians. Since the time of Vatican Council II we have been finding that the great doctrinal controversies of the sixteenth and seventeenth centuries are, to a great extent, not our controversies now, that with patient dialogue we tend to find the common underlying faith beneath them. That discovery engendered great ecumenical hope at the time of the Council, but that hope has faded since as we found that questions of authority and jurisdiction were much harder to broach. No motion seemed to occur in that area until, in his 1995 Encyclical *Ut Unum Sint*, Pope John Paul II made his extraordinary appeal to all the world's Christians to help him in finding how the office of Peter in the Church could better fulfil its task of fostering unity among them. Movingly, he wrote:

This is an immense task, which we cannot refuse and which I cannot carry out by myself. Could not the real but imperfect communion existing between us persuade Church leaders and their theologians to engage with me in a patient and fraternal dialogue on this subject, a dialogue in which, leaving useless controversies behind, we could listen to one another, keeping before us only the will of Christ for his Church and allowing ourselves to be deeply moved by his plea 'that they may all be one . . . so that the world may believe that you have sent me' (John 17.21)?[4]

Between these stumbling blocks to unity, though, on doctrine and authority, there stands this impasse over the recognition of the sacramental character of the various Christian bodies. Our Catholic Church, and the Orthodox even more so, see the sharing of Eucharistic communion as a sign of accomplished full communion between the churches at all levels, whereas Protestants tend more to look for open sacramental communion as the appropriate fulfilment of Christ's command: 'Take this, all of you . . .' If we could reach common agreement on one another's good faith and right faith in this regard, we would have made enormous progress toward the unity of Christians for which Christ prayed.

---

4 Encyclical Letter of Pope John Paul II, *Ut Unum Sint*, 25 May 1995, No. 96. The whole passage on the 'The Ministry of Unity of the Bishop of Rome' is Nos 88–96 and can be found on the website of *La Santa Sede* at http://www.vatican.va/edocs/ENG0221/__PT.HTM

CHAPTER 7

Commitment to the Work of Reconciliation and Peace

Nothing is more emphasized in the Gospels than the measurement of a life of faith, in those who would be followers of Christ, in terms of their readiness to forgive and to pursue the path of reconciliation. Teaching us how to pray, Jesus instructs us to ask: 'Forgive us our trespasses as we forgive those who trespass against us' (Matthew 6.12). Parables such as the one of the unforgiving steward in Matthew 18.23-35, show us God forgiving and demanding that we forgive in return. The father forgives the prodigal son in Luke 15.11-24, and pleads with the jealous elder brother to forgive him as well (vv. 25-32).

When Jesus tells us, 'You, therefore, must be perfect, as your heavenly Father is perfect' (Matthew 5.48), it is at the end of the long sequence of forgiveness requirements in the Sermon on the Mount, and the context is precisely that we are to imitate God our Father in the perfection of his forgiveness.

The parallel text is Luke 6.35-6: 'But love your enemies, do good, and lend, expecting nothing in return; and your reward will be great, and you will be sons of the Most High; for he is kind to the ungrateful and the selfish. Be merciful, even as your Father is merciful'. When it comes to an order of priority, nothing could be clearer than Matthew 5.23-4: 'So if you are offering your gift at the altar, and there remember that your brother has something against you, leave your gift there before the altar and go; first be reconciled to your brother, and then come and offer your gift'.

THE 9/11 MENTALITY IN THE UNITED STATES

On 11 September 2001, the terrorist attacks on New York's World Trade Center and the Pentagon, with yet another attack foiled over the Pennsylvania countryside but doubtless intended to shock us just as much, marked a watershed in our American lives. We have behaved, in many ways, differently since then, conscious of an enemy whose threatening character is constantly borne in upon us, and reacting against this perceived peril. Perhaps in some ways this differs less from the way we behaved before the Cold War broke, when the menace we had so long felt from the Communist bloc so suddenly lifted, and with it the dread of nuclear warfare and the Mutually Assured Destruction (MAD), which it promised.

We had a decade of relief, a brief blossoming of hopes for a peaceful world. It was punctuated of course by the Gulf War and marred by tragedies in the Balkans and Rwanda, but we saw progress in South Africa, in Ireland, and seemingly in the Middle East. 9/11 put an abrupt end to that.

All of us have vivid recollections of that day. I spent that evening sitting on a panel at a local television station, New England Cable News, discussing the event. Some things had become clear to me even over that day; first, of course, that we could not allow such things. Terrorism, which until then had caused its measure of death and destruction, mercifully on a much smaller scale than the terrible wars of the twentieth century, had now graduated to a scale of massive carnage. We could do little more to the nineteen individuals who had carried out this outrage at the cost of their own lives, but others, who either as persons or organizations or even states had supported and encouraged their action, had to be held accountable. Beyond them, though, there existed a sea of anger at the United States and its policies on the part of people who had driven no planes into our towers. How were we to respond to them?

This constituted an unusual situation for the United States. For most of our history we have enjoyed, deservedly or sometimes undeservedly, a startlingly high reputation with the peoples of the world, as a beacon of justice, of liberty, of all the good things that others wished for. We happen not to be seen so in our own time, but viewed instead as agents of much injustice, of the deprivation of freedom, of the monopolization of the goods of the earth, of indifference to the destruction of the planetary environment, of callousness to people's suffering in vast areas of the world.

When I spoke of this on that program on the night of 9/11, another member of the panel, a professor, responded angrily that if people thought so about us, we must make them fear us. Without stopping to think I snapped back at him that I thought the nineteen individuals who had hijacked those planes that day had been trying to do precisely that to us, and I asked: did he want to join them? Not pleased with that answer, this man who had unexpectedly become my adversary replied: we had been taught all these years that we should deal with such animosities by diplomacy, and look where it had got us. Still, I'm afraid, not tempering my own answer with enough respect for him, I retorted: 'Well, our diplomacy must not have been very good'.

And this is the point. If we, as persons or as a nation, do not attend to the grievances of those who act against us and respond to their concerns, we have failed at the most fundamental level of human interaction.

We can put this in terms of recognizing in others the image of God. That is the common heritage of the three Abrahamic religions which unite in basing the dignity of all human persons on their creation in the image of God. It has always impressed me that the most prominent human rights organization in Israel takes the name B'Tselem, 'in the image', from the biblical phrase b'tselem elohim, 'in the image of God'. This yields a basis for human rights broader than the purely individualist one that we have inherited from the eighteenth century Enlightenment.

A PERSONAL EXPERIENCE

I've followed a strange route myself, a voluntary one that cannot oblige anyone else. It embarrasses me to hold my own life experience as a model for anyone else, but I have lived it and learned what I have learned from it. It has had a logic to it which might serve as an example of the labyrinthine ways we come to such things, so I shall allow this last chapter to reflect my very personal experience.

I found myself drawn in 1972 to the conflict in Northern Ireland. I was then a doctoral student at Union Theological Seminary in New York, studying ecumenical theology in the heyday of its popularity right after the Second Vatican Council. Northern Ireland had come to look like the seventeenth century with its struggle between Catholics and Protestants, at a time when I had learned that Protestants were my fellows in Christian faith. Some things had prepared me to walk into this: marching with Dr Martin Luther King, deep opposition to the war in Vietnam, and some years of relating closely to the Rastafarian community in Jamaica at a time when they were scapegoats for anything that went wrong on the island. For motivation, here I was, an ordained Catholic priest. There is no other activity I more enjoy than to say Mass. I stand at the altar and say, in the name of Christ, 'This is my body, which shall be given up for you'. I could not see others, who are body of Christ, Protestant and Catholic, exposed to peril, and not be there with them.

So I went to Northern Ireland in the company of other American theology students, Catholic and Protestant. That we were together, and less threatening to people there because we came from outside their conflict, made it easier to meet people from all parts of both communities, including the armed militant groups of both sides as well as clergy, politicians and neighbourhood people. I made a supposition about the militants, Republican and Loyalist, those who were classified as the 'men of violence', or terrorists, that I was not dealing here with psychopaths, but with people who had put their own lives at risk out of service to their own communities. I could disagree with their judgment that they had no other option than violence, but I had to treat them with respect.

It was my experience that, in every meeting with the Loyalist leadership, the conversation began with their admission that they had done terrible things, and wanted to find another course. With the Irish Republican Army (IRA) it was different. They saw themselves as soldiers, and wanted to be assured that they were fighting a just war. I could never concede this to them until, by the time of their ceasefires, so many years later, they had committed themselves to building an Ireland in which the Protestants, too, could live and be themselves.

Working with people in seemingly endless conflicts, trying

to open up for them, by dint of interpreting their situation, some options to heal their relations, one does get a constant reminder of one's own helplessness and inadequacy. It has always seemed best to me to do this out of the limelight, to deal with the conflicting parties themselves rather than with a public, to publish books or articles only very occasionally. My writing has been mostly direct correspondence with parties in conflict.

A word about method: the interpreting became the essence of my work. What is happening in a conflict seldom resembles what we are reading in the news media. It would be totally presumptuous for the outsider to do the interpretation out of his own head. It can be done only in conversation, fully respect-ful conversation, with all sides in a conflict. People in conflicts typically live in isolation from one another, full of hostile stereotypes of each other but very curious about what makes the other tick. I have generally found it welcome to people in such situations to take part in interpretative conversations that actually include the other side, even if at first it has to be at second hand, through a third party like myself.

But when an understanding of what is happening in a con-flict does come clear, especially to the participants themselves, and expressed in language other than what people have been using, its principal effect is to open up options for action that people had hardly suspected were there.

I have often known people — groups — who have drawn, in hard times, the conclusion that they have no other option but violence, the use of force. I am not inclined to agree with them, as it seems to me an insult to human intelligence that there should be no other options. However I have seen where it can be difficult to discover them, and I have to respect those who, out of conviction, have put their own lives at risk for the sake of their communities, even if they are wrong about it. Given new options other than violence, people of course have to believe that these options are real. But if they are so convinced, everyone, whether conversant with the Just War theory or not, does realize that when there are alternative options the use of force is no longer legitimate.

My own relation to the Northern Irish, developing in ways I could not walk away from, kept me there for the next nine years, living in London but spending a week to two weeks of every month for all those years in Belfast. I have never in fact quit that relation to Northern Ireland in all the thirty-eight years since. When my theology student partners went home after a summer, as I had expected to do myself, I became associated with a most interesting man, an Austrian Jewish Holocaust survivor, Richard Hauser, twenty years my senior, who had been deeply involved for years in the very things that most concerned me. Richard had married Hephzibah Menuhin, the pianist sister to violinist Yehudi Menuhin. Hephzibah travelled regularly on concert tours with Yehudi, but treated her music as her recreation and her work as what she did with Richard and myself, intervening in conflict situations and social crises.

We made a strange trio, and working with them introduced

me into many other conflicts: with both Israelis and Palestinians in the Middle East, as well as with Lebanon and the Kurds of Iraq and Turkey; with the emergence of former colonies in Africa – Angola and Mozambique from Portuguese suzerainty, Rhodesia becoming Zimbabwe, and the liberation of South Africa; with India as it passed through the emergency period under Indira Ghandi; with East Timor suffering Indonesian conquest; with the struggles of dissidents in the Soviet Union. And we were involved, always, with prison reform, with schools, with the elderly and with battered women and children.

My first intuition with the militants of Northern Ireland eventually proved itself, as these movements and organizations, the very ones most involved in the conflict, were themselves the ones that took the major initiatives toward the peace. I had had the experience, for some six weeks during the hunger strike in the prison in 1981, of mediating between the IRA's Army Council and Britain's Northern Ireland Office. Part of my recommendation at that time had been that it be made possible for the prisoners to use the prison as a place to plan the peace. In later years, until the Maze Prison, Long Kesh, was emptied and torn down, I spent much time in its H-Blocks, conversing with prisoners from both sides in sessions that we dignified with the name of 'seminars', about a future of peace.

Decisions had to be made, of course, by the leadership of each organization outside the prison, but the thinking was done there in the cell blocks. People on either side came to the recognition that neither would ever have a satisfactory life in Ireland unless they learned to accommodate the other side. Accommodation sounds a very meagre form of reconciliation, but it had vital importance. The mantra of my own conversations in the prison was that both sides needed to become the guarantors of one another's difference. Eventually there came the ceasefires of 1994 and the process of negotiation that has led to the actual establishment of a functioning power-sharing government in Northern Ireland. The long delay resulted from the fact that those who regarded themselves as the righteous, who had never taken to the gun, were slow to learn that the name of the game was now accommodation. Instead they continued looking for victory over the other side.

One expects the church to have been a factor in all this. In Ireland, the various churches were rather disappointing, and the protagonists, those who were engaged in creating the peace in their organizations and in the prison, had in many cases become thoroughly disillusioned with church. But it was their ingrained disposition of readiness to respect the dignity of the other, a most profound residue of their faith that ultimately guided them past their apprehensions and enmity to that goal of accommodation.

If churches and their leadership had often seemed to have little more to say about the conflict than 'Don't blame us', there were outstanding clerical figures, unfailingly critical but always respectful, who offered genuinely helpful advice and guidance to the militant groups. None was more important than Father Alex Reid of the Clonard Monastery off Belfast's

Falls Road, who gained the respect of the IRA and its leadership and became critically important to its planning of the peace. It is fascinating to learn that, through the mediation of his Redemptorist superiors in Rome and of Archbishop Justin Rigali, at that time Secretary to a Roman Dicastery, Pope John Paul II kept constantly abreast of Alex Reid's work.

On the Protestant side, Presbyterian Minister Roy Magee was of equal importance in his influence with the Loyalist paramilitaries, helping them to create openings for peace. It was he who discovered and encouraged the extraordinary work of prisoner Gusty Spence, convicted of multiple murders, who devoted himself to educating his fellows in the prison in their history, in the character of their own community, and in the opportunities to transform their society into one of peace. Gusty became an important catalyst both for Protestant and for Catholic prisoners.

This fascinating history of the prison in Northern Ireland has its counterpart in what happened on South Africa's Robben Island, the prison located far out in the harbour of Capetown where Nelson Mandela worked with his fellow prisoners at developing the transformative ways of peace, of forgiveness and reconciliation for his country. We may very well be seeing, if we care to look, comparable things happen in the Israeli prisons where political Palestinians — one thinks of Marwan Barghouti — are building consensus now on how to achieve a just peace even as their associates outside the prison war against one another.

THE JESUIT PART OF THIS

That this readiness to seek and find the possibilities of reconciliation in the very people who seem most involved in
their enmities links up with the outlook of the Ignatian
Praesupponendum (already described in Chapter 3 when discussing orthodoxy) must be quite obvious. I have always hoped,
since I knew of it, that this outlook — that it is proper to the
Christian, proper in fact to the human, but indelibly written
into a Christian spirit in particular, to save the proposition of
the other rather than to condemn it as false — would be the
most Jesuit thing about myself.

Ignatius amplifies this to cover all the hard cases, and of
course those are what I primarily encounter. In recent years
I have tended more and more to express that very plainly,
invoking the Ignatian Exercises when I speak with people in
these situations, and I find that it resonates powerfully not
only across the whole Christian spectrum but with Jews and
Muslims and others I meet in these circumstances.

UNDERSTANDING ONE ANOTHER'S
STORIES

It has come to be seen as a truism of such reconciliation
work that we ought to concentrate on storytelling, on hearing people's stories in these conflicts. I've seen this work in

extraordinary ways, as in the case of an Irish volunteer from the Pax Christi organization whom I met in Bosnia in 1998. He had decided that the refugees and displaced persons he worked with so much wanted and needed to have their stories heard that he had devoted himself entirely for several years to recording them; an important service.

When I first began working with people who had suffered the effects of violence in Northern Ireland, I realized that the thing they most desired was the chance to tell their story. They could spin it out all day, and it always told of 'the terrible day', the day when the worst thing in their experience had happened on their street or in their neighbourhood. You could recognize features of the formation of oral tradition, such as the reduction of the experience to mnemonic phrases. If you returned the next day, people wanted to start at the beginning and tell it all over again.

For myself, I found this, at least in part, counter-intuitive over many years. When I first began working with people who had suffered the effects of violence in Northern Ireland I realized that the thing they most desired was the chance to tell their story. They could spin it out all day, and it always told of 'the terrible day', the day when the worst thing in their experience had happened on their street or in their neighbourhood. You could recognize features of the formation of oral tradition, such as the reduction of the experience to mnemonic phrases. If you returned the next day, people wanted to start at the beginning and tell it all over again. While it fulfilled an obvious great need, the process seemed repetitive and sterile. I was always anxious to help people compare their stories with those of others, from other parts of the world where people had found a way to deal with their problems. People would respond very intelligently, for instance, to the experience of Algerians, to that of Black Americans in their civil rights struggle (an important model for the Irish in their own civil rights campaign) or some others. It enabled them to begin dealing with ideas for a future instead of only with the past. Eventually I began to make a distinction between telling the story and making proposals for the future.

That came home to me powerfully when, in 1985, I travelled the Middle East, to Israel and the Arab countries, in a mixed company of American Jews and Christians. In Jordan, we met Khalil al-Wazir, the famous Abu Jihad of the Palestine Liberation Organization (PLO). He invited us very graciously into his house, introduced his wife and daughter, and told us harrowing stories of his own childhood experience. I was transfixed, hearing of his expulsion from his native village, the terrible life of refugee camps, repeated uprootings. I took copious notes.

But as the story went on for what seemed an excessive length of time, with more sufferings in Jordan, sufferings in Egypt, sufferings again in Lebanon, and on and on, I wasn't taking any more notes. I was waiting for something else. Suddenly Hani al-Hassan arrived, the man responsible for all the PLO negotia-tion, always through third parties, with the United States since

1981. Hani gave us up-to-date details of the peace proposals that the PLO, together with King Hussein, was making that year. It was another world, a brighter one.

A few days later, on a Friday, we arrived in Israel, and went together to a synagogue Shabbat service. The Rabbi, thanking us for the effort we were making at this restoration of relations between Arab and Jew, concluded: 'You have heard one side of the story. Now you have to hear the other'.

I knew this would be the first point of the discussion that would follow, and that I had to address it. When the service was done, I opened that session with the recognition: of course we had to hear the other side of the story. In the United States, we in fact heard the Jewish story more commonly than the Arab one, but had still to hear it fully. Yet in Jordan, we had heard not only the story but also the proposal of the peace, and I would be especially interested to hear that in Israel as well.

My own work, in fact, especially since the early 1980s, has concentrated mostly on the Middle East conflict. It has meant much contact, since 1982, with all the many parties, Christian and Muslim, of Lebanon. I have continued my close involvement with Iraqi Kurds and eventually, upon the request, in 1992, of Jalal Talabani, now President of Iraq, with the Kurds of Turkey; and especially, since I began in 1985 to relate very directly to their principal leadership, to Israelis and Palestinians and to the American administrations which have been so necessary a part of all efforts at the resolving of their conflict.

The work in Lebanon required me, for the first time, to work out my own response to Muslim faith. The great priority, for the Catholic Church and in fact for all Christians in the latter twentieth century, of reconciliation with the Jews after the long and dreadful history of Christians persecuting them, had been part of my life long before it had the endorsement of the Second Vatican Council; in fact from my childhood years during the Second World War. Meeting Palestinians in earlier years had never raised the question about Muslims, since Christian and Muslim Palestinians are first agreed on the importance of their being Palestinian, but now I was meeting Christian and Muslim Lebanese in the midst of war.

I had to sort out my response to Islam for myself, existentially as well as theologically, and by the time I had very laboriously done so, I began to realize that most of those around me in Lebanon, Christian or Muslim, had never gone through this exercise or seriously asked themselves these questions. And so a major part of my activity in Lebanon came to be raising these questions. Not until many years later, in 1999, after I had spent considerable time in the countries of the former Yugoslavia, did I write this experience up, at the request of a most remarkable Franciscan Friar, Ivo Marcovic of Sarajevo. Ivo translated my article into Serbo-Croat and published it in a Franciscan quarterly and, in shortened form, in a popular newspaper for the benefit of Croatian and Bosnian Catholics, and it is only in that form that it has ever been published.

RESPECT FOR THE DIGNITY OF THE OTHER

Proposing the peace! Restoring shattered relations among peoples. Building civil relations where they had hardly existed before. Those were early and discouraging days in my own experience of these conflicts. We hardly dared to believe such efforts would succeed. But since then we have seen an astonishing measure of success in the case of Northern Ireland, and may not, for the sake of both parties, allow ourselves to despair of reaching reconciliation, justice and peace in the Israeli–Palestinian conflict.

The key to such success as has been achieved has resided in the recognition of one another and of one another's needs by the conflicting sides. The telling of the story returns. But now it is no longer just the story of pain in the past, but of the discovery of one another, and the planning of the future.

And what of the mediators, of people like myself who try, as third parties, to foster this building or rebuilding of civil relationships? For me, the one most central lesson of any work I have done as mediator in many conflicts is that in seeking to befriend one party to a conflict, we have no need to become the enemy of the other. We can be friends of both, and friends of the peace.

It has been my constant experience, in these situations, that as soon as you approach one side in a conflict, the first demand is that you prove yourself by declaring enmity for the other. Not only is that not necessary, but if we fall into that trap, we become irrelevant to the conflict, merely outsiders butting into a conflict that is not our own, excess baggage to those whose cause we adopt.

One may never neglect questions of justice, or of the imbalance of power which puts one part of a society at the mercy of another. One must always recognize and confront such things, or one becomes the facilitator of injustice. But the confrontation, to be helpful, has to uphold the dignity of all parties. The outsider's role is as catalyst, to discover the options that make a genuine commitment to justice possible for all the parties. I find it an injustice when, as so often happens, the foreign 'observer' or 'helper' turns out to be just another partisan. Commonly such people merely find, in someone else's quarrel, the opportunity to express vicarious anger or frustration over their own quite different problems, impeding the real participants from addressing their needs.

THE ROLE AND THE CO-OPTATION OF RELIGION IN CONFLICTS

As a Catholic priest involved in these concerns, I always look to see if there is a religious content or context of the conflict. When I find it, it is often a kind of rap sheet – negative influences and the use of religion as rationalization for violence. It always interests me to find why this is so, and whether we can expect, from the religions, any positive contribution to healing relations, making the peace.

There are some intrinsic reasons why religion has contributed to divisions and helped to bring about violent conflict. We will come to those. But first I want to comment on an extrinsic reason: the manipulative use of religion for agendas other than its own.

It comes as second nature to many people to ask what use religion may be for some extrinsic purpose, what the churches can do for some cause that we value. Several years ago a group of us from our consortium of theology schools held a conference that brought together theologians and scientists on the subject of ecology, the environment. It soon became apparent that the scientists wanted primarily to know what use was the church for the saving of endangered species, for preventing global warming, for controlling the population explosion, important causes all. We cannot use church or faith that way. Faiths are total outlooks on the world and generate their own agenda. They cannot be used for some other agenda without reductionism, without danger to their very nature. They have to be left to their own devices, and we hope to find that they work to human betterment.

I write that knowing that people are bound to gasp with distrust of the churches and religions, because they have done so badly, damaged human relations, caused enormous and unnecessary suffering, orgies of murderous hate. Some of this certainly comes from the habit of faith communities closing in upon themselves with a total conviction that they are right and everyone else is wrong, but I would argue that instrumental use of religion comes before that as a cause of conflict. Religious institutions seem often to become willing patsies for such uses. We may say that faith is free but religion costs money. Those who have to pay the bills are vulnerable to those who pay the piper and easily agree to serve their purposes.

In Ireland, religion is not altogether about religion. The conflict preceded the Protestant Reformation by some four centuries, with everyone Catholic on all sides, but ever since the Reformation, Catholic and Protestant identities have served as political loyalty tests, and remain so to the present day. One can be genuinely Christian, whether Catholic or Protestant, in Ireland, but if you are Catholic and Unionist, you are a very funny Catholic, and if Protestant and a Nationalist or Republican, you are seen as disloyal to your own people. Constantine, from the moment he first considered granting legal status to Christian religion in his Empire, saw it primarily as a way of bolstering his authority with the help of Christian bishops. Unwittingly, he initiated a power struggle between church and state that generated a whole millennium of wars.

Religion has, for a long time, served as the custodian of the Just War theory. Consequently, every government, when it declares war, calls upon the religious leadership to stand up in the cheering section, the last place they should let themselves be seen in a war, and declare that 'God is on our side'. In the countries of the former Yugoslavia, religion, Christian and Muslim, was commandeered by cynical political leaders to provide the emotional and ideological underpinning for the campaigns of genocide and ethnic cleansing.

It is the commonplace of the Middle East to use religion as a vehicle for rage and frustration. In the fiercely vengeful culture of the contemporary United States, calls for the death penalty, for our massive scale of cruel imprisonment or for cutting off the deprived among us from many forms of public assistance are buttressed by self-righteous appeals to religious superiority. So is the incivility of our treatment of public figures, and of course the religious guerrilla warfare we have described in our own Catholic Church.

Built into almost all religions are doctrines of revelation and election. They can be treated in practically all the religions either as badges of sectarian exclusivity or as opening up human and transcendent possibilities to others. If the latter, we may see those others either as obliged to receive the message under penalty of rejection or, more benignly, as empowered to make choices and let go of their fears in freedom. The more restrictive ways of understanding revelation or election can lead to bitter conflict. These are the intrinsic buttons within the faith traditions that have often led to conflict. But I would contend that more of the instances of religion feeding violent conflict come from its instrumental use for other agendas. Even when the occasion of violence is the claim to exclusive possession of the truth, we can see this, too, as serving the extrinsic agenda of asserting power.

Religions can also carry the cruel image of a wrathful God, one who delights in punishment. In my own perception, this radically distorts the core teaching of any of the familiar faith traditions we are dealing with, and I believe I am at one in this with all but the most reactionary of my theologian colleagues. Forgiveness is a central characteristic of God's action in these traditions.

Yet the cruel God exacting vengeance for every failing appeared commonly in the hard-nosed theologies of the eleventh, twelfth and thirteenth centuries, formative times for our Western law tradition. He lies — unrecognized because we have, since then, de-theologized the law — at the roots of that law tradition in its retributive character. We will not get to a true revision of our concepts of justice without re-examining those tainted roots.

FAITH AS ENGINE OF RECONCILIATION

Can we then expect anything better from the religions?

In the Northern Ireland situation, it became evident to me that many of the people, most of them with experience of violence and prison and who were the creators of the peace process, were thoroughly alienated from their religious roots. They were disillusioned with their churches, as institutions that had failed to do their part, or help to heal the conflict. Nonetheless, they themselves operated out of the principles of reconciliation and readiness to forgive injury that were, or should have been, at the very heart of the religious faith commitment of their churches.

They had the substance, even if their church institutions had not.

We expect that commitment to reconciliation to characterize all of the faith communities. They seem to be strong in theory, weak in practice of that quality.

I write from within the Catholic community of Christian faith, which has great importance to me. I've seen the working of several other faith communities, understood something of their theological positions and the concrete practice of their commitments. I won't try to speak for them on this subject of reconciliation, but commend, to those who live in those other traditions, to examine teaching and practice in this matter of reconciliation within them and explain it to the rest of us.

Within my Christian context, nothing has greater theoretical priority. The Christian Gospel accounts abound in comments on reconciliation, perhaps nowhere more imperatively than in the passage, Matthew 5.23-4, already cited, that tells us to give priority to reconciliation with the brother who has something against us before offering our gift at the altar. Ritual practice can wait, and has no importance comparable to that of reconciliation.

So much for theory. In practice, Christian history has shown us a lot of concern with justice, consistently retributive justice. We hear far less of reconciliation or the practice of forgiveness that the Gospels so much urge. But a peculiar thing happened to the practice of reconciliation in Christian history. It disappeared into the confessional and became exclusively the forgiveness of our personal sins by God.

143

In this way it was privatized, made exclusively a matter between me and Jesus. Reconciliation with the brother, the sister, the neighbour tended to be lost in the shuffle. Especially the public character of reconciliation and forgiveness, the reestablishment of wholeness in the relations between nations and peoples, failed to become a focus in the life of the faith community. Concepts of retribution and compulsion reigned supreme in all those public areas.

THE SACRED AND THE SECULAR

Is this still true for us? What we have lived through in this last century has been the bloodiest period of human history. The concerns touched in this last chapter may sound very secular, but they are at the heart of our faith tradition. Indeed, we often best understand the most extraordinary and paradoxical demands of our faith — love of enemies, taking up the cross and following Christ, saving our life only as we lose it — when we see them in the secular contexts that we really live with. It is there that we join the exercise of the healing mission of Christ, that we let ourselves be witness, by our lives, to the enduring presence of Christ, his love, his mercy and his forgiveness in the world.

Index

145